SpringerBriefs in Information Security and Cryptography

The series aims to develop and disseminate an understanding of innovations, paradigms, techniques, and technologies in the contexts of information and cybersecurity systems, as well as developments in cryptography and related studies.

It publishes concise, thorough and cohesive overviews of state-of-the-art topics in these fields, as well as in-depth case studies. The series also provides a single point of coverage of advanced and timely, emerging topics and offers a forum for core concepts that may not have reached a level of maturity to warrant a comprehensive monograph or textbook.

It addresses security, privacy, availability, and dependability issues, also welcoming emerging technologies such as artificial intelligence, cloud computing, cyber physical systems, and big data analytics related to cybersecurity research. Among some core research topics:

Fundamentals and theories

- Cryptography for cybersecurity
- Theories of cybersecurity
- Provable security

Cyber Systems and Secure Networks

- Cyber systems security
- Network security
- Security services
- Social networks security and privacy
- Cyber attacks and defense
- Data-driven cyber security
- Trusted computing and systems

Applications and others

- Hardware and device security
- Cyber application security
- Human and social aspects of cybersecurity

Stephan Krenn · Thomas Lorünser

An Introduction to Secret Sharing

A Systematic Overview and Guide for Protocol Selection

 Springer

Stephan Krenn
Center for Digital Safety and Security
AIT Austrian Institute of Technology
Wien, Austria

Thomas Lorünser
Center for Digital Safety and Security
AIT Austrian Institute of Technology
Wien, Austria

ISSN 2731-9555   ISSN 2731-9563 (electronic)
SpringerBriefs in Information Security and Cryptography
ISBN 978-3-031-28160-0   ISBN 978-3-031-28161-7   (eBook)
https://doi.org/10.1007/978-3-031-28161-7

This Springer imprint is published by the registered company Springer Nature Switzerland AG
The registered company address is: Gewerbestrasse 11, 6330 Cham, Switzerland

Preface

The continuing trend towards cloudification is accompanied by increasing awareness of users for data privacy and confidentiality. What is therefore needed are provably secure mechanisms to outsource potentially sensitive data into the cloud, thereby taking into consideration long-term confidentiality, availability, and integrity of the stored data. Secret sharing offers a viable solution to this challenge, by letting a user locally fragment her data into numerous shares, such that only predefined subsets of these shares can be used to reconstruct the data, while any other set of shares does not reveal anything—potentially even in an information theoretic sense. By distributing the different shares to different storage providers, users can now benefit from the high availability guarantees of cloud services, without leaking anything about their data or having to bother about key management challenges in case of collaboratively shared resources.

After having first been introduced in the late 1970s, secret sharing has been an active field of research ever since. Over the last decades, a number of different schemes have been introduced, satisfying different security goals, achieving different levels of efficiency, and offering different advanced features and functionalities. With this book, we aim at a systematic overview of the state of the art, thereby providing a guide for protocol selection for specific scenarios and use cases. We therefore present the different security models, motivate their needs, and provide efficient instantiations for each of those models. Furthermore, we provide the reader with extensive references to the scientific literature to allow for deep-diving into the cryptographic literature in order to identify the correct schemes for every application domain.

Vienna, Austria
March 2023

Stephan Krenn
Thomas Lorünser

Acknowledgements

The research leading to this work has been co-funded by the European Union's Horizon 2020 research and innovation program under Grant Agreements No 644962 (Prismacloud) and No 830929 (CyberSec4Europe), as well as the Digital Europe Programme under Grant Agreement No 101091642 (Qci-Cat).

Views and opinions expressed are however those of the authors only and do not necessarily reflect those of the European Union or the European Commission. Neither the European Union nor the granting authority can be held responsible for them.

The authors would like to thank their colleagues, including but not limited to, Denise Demirel, Andreas Happe, Sebastian Ramacher, Daniel Slamanig, Christoph Striecks, Guilia Traverso, and Florian Wohner, for valuable discussions and inputs when editing earlier versions of this work.

Contents

Chapter 1
Introduction

Cloud computing is one of the most important growth areas in ICT and is at the heart of many cyber-physical systems and smart applications. Although not a fundamentally new technology from a computer science perspective, it is fundamentally changing the delivery models for IT resources and services, i.e., the way we use computing and storage resources and software solutions. Large cloud infrastructures enable on-demand self-service of infrastructure, platform and services at a very competitive price and on a pay-per-use basis. This can optimize many business opportunities and helps to increase innovation capacity. However, in most cases this IT delivery model also means adopting an outsourcing model with all the associated problems from a security perspective. Running business-critical processes on shared infrastructures without direct control introduces many new risks and requires new safeguards to mitigate the corresponding threats.

Data breaches and data loss are two of the biggest risks in cloud use that discourage many stakeholders from using this technology. Naïve encryption solutions only protect the confidentiality of data, but do not address the risk of data loss; rather, they introduce further risks in the event of a lost or destroyed decryption key. Moreover, simple encrypt-then-store solutions do not scale well with the number of users, especially in the case of highly dynamic groups sharing a large number of files with different access rights, due to key management challenges.

In this book, we therefore explore techniques for distributed storage systems that simultaneously protect against data breach and data loss. We consider possible solutions for storage systems based on secret sharing, a versatile cryptographic primitive that is ideal as a secure data distribution algorithm. The application of threshold secret sharing allows data to be encrypted into multiple parts, so that only a predefined number of parts are required to recover the information. While the naïve application of secret sharing algorithms seems straightforward, a more detailed analysis reveals many difficulties and limitations that need to be considered and addressed in cloud-of-cloud environments.

This book is dedicated to survey the available secret sharing techniques and categorize them according to their properties. We distinguish them according to the confidentiality properties they provide (information theoretically secure vs. com-

S. Krenn and T. Lorünser, *An Introduction to Secret Sharing*,
SpringerBriefs in Information Security and Cryptography,
https://doi.org/10.1007/978-3-031-28161-7_1

putationally secure), the network model they are designed for (synchronous vs. asynchronous), and the protocol-level properties they support. We provide a comprehensive analysis of the state-of-the-art primitives for secret sharing and present the most efficient protocols with respect to typical requirements encountered when building a secure and privacy-preserving data sharing solution in a cloud-of-clouds environment.

1.1 A Primer on Secret Sharing

Consider a user who wishes to store potentially private data in the cloud. As the user does not have direct control over the storage servers, they need to be considered potentially untrusted and unreliable, so that availability and confidentiality are not immediately guaranteed.

While simply encrypting the data and storing it redundantly on multiple servers might seem like a trivial solution to this problem, it causes severe issues regarding key management as soon as a user wants to access his data from multiple devices, or share data with other users. For instance, to achieve fine grained access control in the latter case, each file would need to be encrypted under a different key which could then be given to those who are granted access, or computationally more expensive primitives like attribute based encryption schemes [117] or proxy re-encryption schemes [18] need to be deployed. Finally, this approach only guarantees security against a computationally bounded adversary, which might be problematic, e.g., for electronic health records, where long term privacy matters. This would require to estimate the computational power of an adversary in the far future, which is very problematic, not least given Shor's quantum algorithm to break most number theoretic cryptographic schemes [124], and recent breakthroughs in quantum computing, e.g., [134].

Alternatively, a user can split the secret data into multiple shares, and then store one of these shares per storage provider. However, in contrast to a local RAID system, the sharing is performed in a way that guarantees that the single shares to not reveal any information about the original data. Even more, this approach can be instantiated in an information theoretically secure way: as long as the adversary is not able to corrupt a sufficiently large set of servers, he cannot infer any information about the stored data – independent of his computational resources. In contrast to the encrypt-then-duplicate approach, this solution works without any keys, and thus complex key management can be fully avoided. On the other hand, it is important to note that the trust model is fundamentally different in this case, as security is guaranteed under a *non-collusion assumption*, meaning that confidentiality holds as long as no more than a predefined number of servers pool their shares; in case that this assumption is violated, the colluding servers can efficiently recover the secret data. Although this seems easy to understand in the first place, application in real use cases is not straightforward as shown in [67], because many parameters and constraints have an influence on good configurations.

Secret sharing schemes achieving this goals were first introduced independently by Blakely [16] and Shamir [123]. It allows a *dealer* to distribute some secret s among a set of parties (or servers) $\mathcal{P} = \{P_1, \ldots, P_n\}$, such that every designated *qualified subset* of $\mathcal{P}$ can efficiently recompute s, while all other sets of parties do not learn any information about s.

A bit more formally, in a secret sharing scheme one defines an *access structure* $\Gamma \subseteq 2^{\mathcal{P}}$ defining all qualified sets in the system. For obvious reasons, we will only consider the case where adding an additional party to a qualified set always result in a qualified set as well. For secret data s in the domain of the scheme, the dealer $D \notin \mathcal{P}$ now computes a share σ_i for each P_i, such that s can efficiently be recomputed from a set $\{\sigma_i\}_{i \in I}$ if and only if $I \in \Gamma$, while no information about s is revealed otherwise.

The arguable most important access structures are so-called *threshold access structures*, where a set $S \subseteq \mathcal{P}$ is qualified if and only if it contains at least k parties for some fixed threshold $k \leq n$. Intuitively, this means that every server is equally important for reconstruction, and that all servers are equally trusted by the dealer. We believe that this a natural assumption in the case of distributed storage, as more trusted servers would immediately become more valuable also for an attacker, which in turn would reduce their trustworthiness.

Intuitively, in the case that $k = n$, i.e., that all servers are required for reconstruction, a secret s can simply be shared by choosing random σ_i such that $s = \sigma_1 + \cdots + \sigma_n$, where the computations are carried out in some finite group, cf. also Section 4.1.1.

In the following chapters, we will present various schemes for different types of access structures, including threshold access structures and beyond. In the selection of the presented schemes, we focused on schemes achieving high storage efficiency, i.e., keeping the size of the individual shares as small as possible.

1.2 Applications

In the following we discuss two representative application scenarios for secret sharing in more detail.

1.2.1 Distributed Storage

The application of secret sharing in the context of multi-cloud storage applications is one which is one of the most evident use cases. The idea of secure distributed storage was already introduced in the original work of Rabin when he introduced information dispersal [112] or also Shamir, who presented the first information-theoretically secure scheme [123]. Moreover, various practical implementations have been demonstrated in [?, 81, 98, 122] since then.

As described above, a user would locally share the secret data and then send the resulting shares to different storage providers. The advantages of this approach compared to a encrypt-then-store approach can be summarized as follows [97]:

Improved data confidentiality and availability: Distributing data using threshold secret sharing schemes improves both confidentiality and availability. One the one hand, this is because the data cannot be accessed in the plain as long as no sufficiently large number of servers colludes. Furthermore, secret sharing is the only known information-theoretically secure method for protecting data at rest, i.e., the best candidate for building long-term secure systems. On the other hand, availability comes from the fact that only a fraction of the shares is needed to restore the original data, i.e., reconstruction succeeds even if $n - k$ servers are unavailable. That is, secret sharing directly incorporates adjustable levels of redundancy, also increasing the resilience of higher-level applications.

Reduced storage overhead: Computationally secure secret sharing can significantly reduce the total data storage capacity required to achieve a given level of availability compared to traditional replication strategies. Figure 1.1 compares the total amount of data used with a simple replication strategy. The benefit becomes more significant when the number of nodes increases.

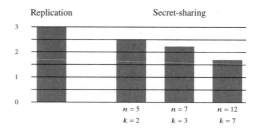

Fig. 1.1 Comparison of required redundancy to achieve 99.9% availability when every server has 90% availability, assuming independent failures. Redundancy requirements cannot be lower than 1 (corresponding to the original data size).

Avoidance of vendor lock-ins: The system is essentially based on standard technologies and allows interaction of different storage vendors. The technology itself is independent of storage service offerings. The use of published and well-documented algorithms is essential to allow for an easy migration from one storage location to another.

Keyless operation: Compared to standard encryption methods, secret sharing enables keyless modes of operation. Security is determined by the non-collision of the parties holding the shares, rather than by the private key. The absence of a key eliminates the need for complex key management, which is very useful in many cases, although credentials are still usually required to manage access to the storage locations. However, the practical significance of security based on non-collusion assumptions remains controversial.

1.2.2 Multiparty Computation

Besides pure storage applications, secret sharing can also be extended to perform privacy-preserving computations on outsourced data using so-called secure multi-party computation (MPC), allowing for more versatile collaboration scenarios on the data [20, 90, 99, 100, 139].

Multiparty computation (MPC) is a technology for computing on encrypted data in a distributed environment, i.e., with multiple nodes that only have secure fragments of input data and do not learn anything from them. The concept was developed more than 30 years ago, and a large amount of research has been done on the subject over the last three decades. For a long time it was considered only theoretical, but advances in recent years have led to many interesting applications that can be realized with practical efficiency if implemented appropriately. In principle, MPC can be used to decentralize systems that typically require a central trusted authority to perform certain functions. The function is then evaluated jointly by multiple parties, guaranteeing the correctness of the output and preserving the privacy of each party's input; only the output of the computation becomes known.

More specifically, in secure multiparty computation (MPC) a set of parties can jointly evaluate a function without leaking information to any of the participating parties, beyond what they can derive from their own inputs and the result of the computation. Interestingly, information-theoretically secure MPC exists and is based on secret sharing — as introduced by Ben-Or et al. [9] and Chaum et al. [42]. Thus, it is possible to obliviously compute arbitrary functions on secret shared data providing long-term security. The respective class of MPC protocols with information-theoretic security operates in the honest majority setting, i.e., under the assumption that an adversary corrupts less than half of the MPC computing nodes. Besides the non-collusion assumption, the protocols also rely on secure channels, which can be assured by different means.

Multiparty computation provides *input secrecy* (or *input privacy*), i.e., no party learns the input values of any other party, and *correctness*, i.e., the receiver of the result is ensured that the result is correct. Fortunately, information-theoretically secure MPC protocols are among the most performant approaches for computing on encrypted data and achieve practical performance in many application scenarios.

Additionally, also the category of dishonest majority MPC protocols in the spirit of SPDZ [51, 52] rely on information-theoretic secret sharing at the core in combination with an information-theoretic mac. However, they use beaver triple based [5] multiplication techniques, which require an additional offline pre-computation phase to generate the beaver triples, i.e., valid sharings of random values a, b and c such that $c = a \cdot b$, which can only be generated by dedicated protocols on the basis of somewhat homomorphic encryption or oblivious transfer, which can only be realized from asymmetric primitives.

Chapter 2
Preliminaries

In this section, we first introduce some notation that will be used throughout this introduction to secret sharing. Subsequently, we will recap basic cryptographic primitives that are needed as building blocks for the schemes presented later on. Readers familiar with the basic concepts of cryptography can safely skip this chapter upon first reading, and come back to it whenever needed.

2.1 Notation

We denote algorithms by sans serif fonts such as A, B. Sets are denoted by calligraphic fonts, e.g., $\mathcal{S}, \mathcal{T}$. The set of integers is written as $\mathbb{Z}$; $\mathbb{Z}_q := \mathbb{Z}/q\mathbb{Z}$ denotes the additive group of integers modulo q, and $\mathbb{Z}_q^*$ denotes the multiplicative group modulo q. For a set $\mathcal{S}$, $2^{\mathcal{S}}$ is the power set of $\mathcal{S}$, i.e., the set consisting of all subsets of $\mathcal{S}$. The cardinality of $\mathcal{S}$ is denoted by $|\mathcal{S}|$, and the length of a string s by $|s|$.

For a set $\mathcal{S}$, $s \xleftarrow{\$} \mathcal{S}$ denotes that s was chosen uniformly at random from $\mathcal{S}$. For an algorithm A, $s \xleftarrow{\$} $ A means that s was the output of A with fresh random coins. We use the notation $\Pr[\mathcal{E} : \Omega]$ to denote the probability of event $\mathcal{E}$ over the probability space Ω. For example, $\Pr\left[f(x) = 1 : x \xleftarrow{\$} \{0,1\}^n\right]$ is the probability that $f(x) = 1$ for a uniformly drawn x in $\{0,1\}^n$.

An algorithm is said to be PPT (probabilistic polynomial time), if it is a probabilistic algorithm whose runtime is bounded above by a polynomial in the input length.

We use standard Big O notation to describe the behavior of functions. In particular, we write $f(n) = O(g(n))$, if $f(n)$ is asymptotically bounded above by $g(n)$, i.e., there exists a constant $c > 0$ such that for all sufficiently large n it holds that $|f(n)| \leq c|g(n)|$. Conversely, we write $f(n) = \Omega(g(n))$, if $f(n)$ is asymptotically bounded below by $g(x)$, i.e., there exists a constant $c > 0$ such that for all sufficiently large n it holds that $f(n) \geq cg(n)$. We further write $\tilde{O}, \tilde{\Omega}, \dots$ if the relations hold up to logarithmic factors.

© The Author(s), under exclusive license to Springer Nature Switzerland AG 2023
S. Krenn and T. Lorünser, *An Introduction to Secret Sharing*,
SpringerBriefs in Information Security and Cryptography,
https://doi.org/10.1007/978-3-031-28161-7_2

We say that a function $\mathsf{negl}(n)$ is *negligible* (in n), if it vanishes faster than every inverse polynomial. That is, for every integer $k > 0$ there exists an integer n_k such that for all $n > n_k$ it holds that $\mathsf{negl}(n) < n^{-k}$.

By $\log(n)$, we denote the logarithm of n in base 2.

Finally, the main security parameter will be denoted by λ.

2.2 Mathematical Background and Complexity Assumptions

Before recapitulating the necessary complexity assumptions, we briefly recap some basic mathematical concepts.

A group can be thought of as a direct generalization of the integers:

Definition 2.1 Let G be a set and $\otimes$ be a binary operation on elements of G. The pair $\mathcal{G} = (G, \otimes)$ is called a *group* if and only if the following conditions are satisfied:

- **Closure:** For all $a, b \in G$ it holds that $a \otimes b \in G$.
- **Associativity:** For all $a, b, c \in G$ we have that $(a \otimes b) \otimes c = a \otimes (b \otimes c)$.
- **Identity element:** There exists $e \in G$ such that $a \otimes e = e \otimes a = a$ for all $a \in G$. The (unique) element e is called the *identity element*.
- **Inverse element:** For every $a \in G$ there exists $b \in G$ such that $a \otimes b = b \otimes a = e$. The (unique) element b is called the *inverse* of a.

The group $\mathcal{G}$ is further said to be *abelian* or *commutative*, if in addition the following condition is satisfied:

- **Commutativity:** For all $a, b \in G$ we have that $a \otimes b = b \otimes a$.

For an element $g \in G$, we will write g^n for an integer n to denote $g \otimes \cdots \otimes g$ (n times).

Most groups considered in the following will have a special structure, in the sense that they can be generated by a single element:

Definition 2.2 Let $\mathcal{G}$ be a group and $g \in \mathcal{G}$, and let $\langle g \rangle = \{g^i : i \in \mathbb{Z}\}$. The element g is called a *generator* of the group, if and only if $\langle g \rangle = \mathcal{G}$. The group is said to be *cyclic* if and only if such a g exists.

Definition 2.3 Let G be a group and $g \in G$. The smallest positive integer n satisfying $g^n = 1$ is called the *order* of g and is denoted by $n = \mathrm{ord}(g)$. If no such n exists, then g is said to have infinite order. The order of $\mathcal{G}$ is its cardinality, i.e., $\mathrm{ord}(\mathcal{G}) = |\mathcal{G}|$. A group is called *finite*, if $\mathrm{ord}(\mathcal{G}) < \infty$.

With this, we are no able to define one of the most central computational problems in modern cryptography:

Definition 2.4 Let $\mathcal{G}$ be finite cyclic group, and let g be a generator of $\mathcal{G}$. Given $h \in \mathcal{G}$, the *discrete logarithm problem* is to find an integer x satisfying $h = g^x$ (x is called the *discrete logarithm* of h in base g, denoted by $x = \log_g h$).

In the remainder of this book, we will often make specific assumptions about the groups we are operating in. In particular, we will often require that the *discrete logarithm assumption* holds in a specific group G. That is, we will assume that given a generator g of G and a random $h \in G$, no PPT algorithm can solve the discrete logarithm problem with more than negligible (in $\log(\mathrm{ord}\,G)$) probability.

For a fully formal definition, we refer, e.g., to Katz and Lindell [89].

2.3 Basic Cryptographic Primitives

In the following we give a brief overview of those cryptographic primitives that will be used as building blocks in the remainder of this book. For comprehensive discussions on the presented primitives, variants on their security definitions, and instantiations we refer to the original literature.

2.3.1 Hash Functions

A hash function Hash is an efficiently computable function mapping strings of arbitrary finite length to elements of a fixed and finite set. In the following, we will assume that all hash functions are *preimage resistant* and *collision resistant*. Informally, the former means that given a value h in the co-domain of Hash, it is computationally infeasible to find an input that maps to h, i.e., it is hard to find $M \in \{0, 1\}^*$ such that $h = \mathrm{Hash}(M)$. The latter means that it is computationally infeasible to find two inputs mapping to the same hash value, i.e., no efficient adversary can come up with $M_0 \neq M_1 \in \{0, 1\}^*$ such that $\mathrm{Hash}(M_0) = \mathrm{Hash}(M_1)$. For formal definitions we refer, e.g., to Rogaway and Shrimpton [115].

For concreteness, the reader may simply think of SHA-2 or SHA-3.

2.3.2 Symmetric Encryption Schemes

A symmetric encryption scheme allows two parties to communicate in a confidential way. In such a scheme, the two parties share a common key, which is used for both, encryption and decryption. On a high level, a symmetric encryption scheme is said to be secure, if no adversary can tell the content of a ciphertext, even if it has access to encryptions of arbitrary messages of its own choice.

For concreteness, the reader may simply think of state-of-the-art symmetric encryption schemes such as AES, Serpent, or Twofish.

Definition 2.5 A *symmetric encryption scheme* with key space $\mathcal{K}$, message space $\mathcal{M}$, and ciphertext space C consists of a pair of algorithms (Enc, Dec):

Experiment $\text{Exp}_{\mathsf{A}}^{\text{IND-CPA}}$:

$\quad b \xleftarrow{\$} \{0, 1\}$

$\quad K \xleftarrow{\$} \mathcal{K}$

$\quad (M_0, M_1, \mathsf{st}) \xleftarrow{\$} \mathsf{A}(1^\lambda)^{O(\cdot, K)}$

$\quad\quad\quad\quad$ where, on input $M \in \mathcal{M}$, O behaves as follows:

$\quad\quad\quad\quad\quad\quad$ return $\mathsf{Enc}(M, K)$

$\quad C \xleftarrow{\$} \mathsf{Enc}(M_b, K)$

$\quad b' \xleftarrow{\$} \mathsf{A}(\mathsf{st}, C)^{O(\cdot, K)}$

$\quad$ return $(b \stackrel{?}{=} b') \ \wedge \ (|M_0| \stackrel{?}{=} |M_1|)$

Fig. 2.1 The IND-CPA experiment $\text{Exp}_{\mathsf{A}}^{\text{IND-CPA}}$

Enc: On input a key $K \in \mathcal{K}$ and a message $M \in \mathcal{M}$, this algorithm outputs a ciphertext $C \in C$.

Dec: On input a key $K \in \mathcal{K}$ and a ciphertext $C \in C$, this algorithm outputs a message $M \in \mathcal{M}$.

The algorithms further satisfy the following security properties:

Completeness: Decryption of a ciphertext always yields the original plaintext. That is, for every key $K \in \mathcal{K}$ and every message $M \in \mathcal{M}$, it holds that:

$$\Pr\left[M = M' : M' \xleftarrow{\$} \mathsf{Dec}(K, \mathsf{Enc}(K, M))\right] = 1$$

IND-CPA Security: The ciphertext does not reveal any information about the plaintext, no matter how many plaintext/ciphertext pairs the adversary knows. That is, for every PPT algorithm A there exists a negligible function negl such that the following holds:

$$\Pr\left[\text{Exp}_{\mathsf{A}}^{\text{IND-CPA}} = 1\right] \leq \frac{1}{2} + \mathsf{negl}(\lambda),$$

where the experiment is defined in Figure 2.1.

For convenience, we will sometimes write $\mathsf{Enc}_K(M)$ instead of $\mathsf{Enc}(K, M)$, and similarly for Dec. In-depth discussions can be found, e.g., in [89].

2.3.3 Message Authentication Codes

A *message authentication code* (or MAC for short) is a short bitstring that can be used to authenticate a message, i.e., to prove its integrity and authenticity.

A MAC can be thought of as a symmetric version of digital signatures: both, the sender and the receiver of a message share a secret key. When the sender wants to "sign" a message, he uses this key to compute the *tag* which is then appended to the message. The receiver checks the authenticity of the message by simply recomputing the tag, and comparing it to the received value. A MAC is said to be secure, if it is infeasible to compute a tag on a new message without knowing the corresponding secret key. Note here that all MACs considered in the following are assumed to be deterministic.

The following definition follows the presentation of Cevallos et al. [38].

Definition 2.6 A *message authentication code (MAC)* for a finite message space $\mathcal{M}$ consists of an algorithm Mac : $\mathcal{M} \times \mathcal{K} \to \mathcal{T}$, where the key space $\mathcal{K}$ and the tag space $\mathcal{T}$ are both finite. It is called ε*-secure*, if for all $m, m' \in \mathcal{M}$ satisfying $m \neq m'$, and for all $\tau, \tau' \in \mathcal{T}$, it holds that:

$$\Pr\left[\mathsf{Mac}(m', K) = \tau' \mid \mathsf{Mac}(m, K) = \tau\right] \leq \varepsilon .$$

Here, the probability space is taken over all possible choices of the key $K \in \mathcal{K}$.

For notational convenience, we will sometimes write $\mathsf{Mac}_K(m)$ instead of $\mathsf{Mac}(m, K)$.

2.3.4 Commitment Schemes

A commitment scheme allows a party to commit to a certain value without revealing it, while having the possibility to open the commitment at some later point in time in a unique way. A commitment can thus be thought of as a locked box containing a message chosen by some party. The box (but not the key) is then given to the other party, and thus the first one is not able to alter the message any more. However, the receiver of the box cannot access the message until the committer decides to open it using its key.

Definition 2.7 A *commitment scheme* for message space $\mathcal{M}$ is a triple of PPT algorithms (KGen, Commit, Verify):

KGen: This generation algorithm outputs a public commitment key K on input 1^λ.
Commit: Taking a public commitment key K and a message $M \in \mathcal{M}$ as an input, this algorithm outputs a pair (c, d), which is a commitment/opening pair for m.
Verify: Given a commitment key K, a message M, a commitment c and an opening d, this algorithm either outputs a bit indicating whether to accept or to reject the opening.

The algorithms further have to satisfy the following security properties:

Completeness: An honestly computed commitment is always accepted in the verification algorithm. That is, for all messages $M \in \mathcal{M}$ it holds that:

$$\Pr\left[b = 1 : \begin{array}{c} K \xleftarrow{\$} \mathsf{KGen}(1^\lambda), (c, d) \xleftarrow{\$} \mathsf{Commit}(K, M), \\ b \xleftarrow{\$} \mathsf{Verify}(K, M, c, d) \end{array}\right] = 1 .$$

Hiding: A commitment does not reveal information about the contained messages.
That is, for every PPT algorithm A there exists a negligible function negl such
that:

$$\Pr\left[b = b' : \begin{array}{c} b \xleftarrow{\$} \{0,1\}, K \xleftarrow{\$} \mathsf{KGen}(1^\lambda), \\ (M_0, M_1, \mathsf{st}) \xleftarrow{\$} \mathsf{A}(K, 1^\lambda), \\ (c,d) \xleftarrow{\$} \mathsf{Commit}(K, M_b), b' \xleftarrow{\$} \mathsf{A}(\mathsf{st}, c) \end{array}\right] \le \frac{1}{2} + \mathsf{negl}(\lambda).$$

Binding: No adversary should be able to change his mind about the message after
having sent the commitment. That is, for every PPT adversary A there exists a
negligible function negl such that:

$$\Pr\left[\begin{array}{c} M_0, M_1 \ne \bot \wedge \\ b_0 = b_1 = 1 \end{array} : \begin{array}{c} K \xleftarrow{\$} \mathsf{KGen}(1^\lambda), \\ (c, d_0, d_1, M_0, M_1) \xleftarrow{\$} \mathsf{A}(K, 1^\lambda), \\ b_0 = \mathsf{Verify}(K, M_0, c, d_0), \\ b_1 = \mathsf{Verify}(K, M_1, c, d_1) \end{array}\right] \le \mathsf{negl}(\lambda).$$

A commitment scheme is called *perfectly hiding*, if negl = 0 for the hiding property,
and similarly *perfectly binding* if negl = 0 for the binding property. It is easy to
see that no commitment scheme can be perfectly hiding and perfectly binding at the
same time.

Pedersen [111] introduced a very simple commitment scheme which we describe
next.

KGen: On input 1^λ, this algorithm outputs a prime q according to [75] and a group
$\mathcal{G}$ of order q in which the discrete logarithm assumption holds. Furthermore, it
outputs two random generators g, h of $\mathcal{G}$ such that nobody knows $\log_g h$ or vice
versa. The message space is given by $\mathbb{Z}_q$.

Commit: Given a message $M \in \mathbb{Z}_q$, this algorithm draws $r \xleftarrow{\$} \mathbb{Z}_q$ and outputs
$(c, d) = (g^M h^r, r)$.

Verify: This algorithm outputs 1, if and only if $c = g^M h^d$.

Theorem 2.1 *The Pedersen commitment scheme is perfectly hiding and computationally binding if the discrete logarithm assumption holds in $\mathcal{G}$.*

Proof Completeness is straightforward to see. To see the perfect hiding property,
note that because of $\langle g \rangle = \langle h \rangle = \mathcal{G}$, the blinding factor h^r is a uniformly random
element in $\mathcal{G}$, and therefore perfectly blinds g^M. Finally, assume that an adversary
would find $(M_0, r_0) \ne (M_1, r_1)$ such that $g^{M_0} h^{r_0} = g^{M_1} h^{r_1}$. Then we would have
$g^{M_0 - M_1} = h^{r_1 - r_0}$, or $g = h^{(r_1 - r_0)(M_0 - M_1)^{-1}}$, where the inversion is modulo q. But
this means that the adversary was able to compute $\log_g h = (r_1 - r_0)(M_0 - M_1)^{-1}$
mod q which is hard by assumption.   □

2.3.5 Zero-Knowledge Proofs of Knowledge

A zero-knowledge proof of knowledge is a two-party protocol between a prover and a verifier, which allows the prover to convince the verifier that it knows some secret piece of information without revealing it. The primitive was first introduced by Goldwasser et al. [76], and the definitions were later refined by Bellare and Goldreich [7]. The following description is based on Bichsel et al. [12].

Zero-knowledge proofs of knowledge have to satisfy the following security properties. First, *correctness* says that honest provers can always convince honest verifiers. Furthermore, they have to satisfy the following seemingly contradictory goals: On the one hand, *soundness* guarantees that a prover that can convince the verifier really knows the claimed secret, except for a negligibly small probability. On the other hand, the *zero-knowledge* property says that the proof does not reveal any information about the secret to the verifier, except for what is already revealed by the claim itself.

What is typically being proved in our applications is knowledge of discrete logarithms or similar statements. Now and in the following we use the notation introduced by Camenisch and Stadler [33] to denote such proof in an abstract way. For instance, an expression like:

$$\mathsf{ZKP}\left[(\alpha, \beta) \ : \ y = g^\alpha h^\beta\right], \tag{2.1}$$

denotes a zero-knowledge proof of knowledge of integers α, β such that the relation on the right hand side are satisfied. We stick to the convention that knowledge of values denoted by Greek letters has to be proved, while all other values are assumed to be publicly known.

Figure 2.2 illustrates the protocol run for this proof goal. Let therefore g and h be generators of a group $\mathcal{G}$ of prime order q. Let further be Hash a collision resistant hash function (formally modelled as a random oracle), and $\mathsf{desc}_\mathcal{G}$ be a description of the group $\mathcal{G}$.

Prover	Verifier
$r_a, r_b \xleftarrow{\$} \mathbb{Z}_q$	
$t := g^{r_a} h^{r_b}$	
$c := \mathsf{Hash}(t; y, g, h, \mathsf{desc}_\mathcal{G})$	
$s_a := r_a + c\alpha$	
$s_b := r_b + c\beta$	

$$\xrightarrow{\quad (c, (s_a, s_b)) \quad}$$

$$t' := g^{s_a} h^{s_b} y^{-c}$$

Output 1 if and only if:

$$c \stackrel{?}{=} \mathsf{Hash}(t'; y, g, h, \mathsf{desc}_\mathcal{G})$$

Fig. 2.2 Protocol flow of the zero-knowledge proof of knowledge specified in (2.1).

In abuse of notation, we will also use the notation from (2.1) to only denote the prover's algorithm, i.e., $\pi \xleftarrow{\$} \mathsf{ZKP}[\ldots]$ will denote the message output by the prover.

For a deeper discussion of the design of efficient zero-knowledge proofs of knowledge for practically relevant proof goals we refer the interested reader to the original literature, in particular Schnorr [118] and generalizations [32, 50, 68], and Fiat and Shamir [65]. A detailed discussion can also be found in Bangerter et al. [4].

Chapter 3
Adversary Models for Secret Sharing Schemes

As already mentioned, the basic security requirement for secret sharing schemes is that no unqualified set of share holders must be able to gain any information about the shared secret. However, there are subtle differences regarding the computational power of a potential adversary that need to be considered, e.g., whether it is computationally bounded or not, or whether it may have access to a quantum computer or not.

Furthermore, besides this basic privacy requirement, different schemes found in the literature offer a variety of additional features, e.g., to protect against actively malicious servers cheating at reconstruction time, or to detect (potentially unintentionally) malicious dealers distributing inconsistent shares.

In the following we therefore briefly describe the most important types of adversaries considered in the literature, in the dimensions of *computational power*, as well as its capabilities on the *network layer* and *protocol level*.

3.1 Computational Power

Regarding the computational power, one typically only distinguish adversaries which are either computationally bounded or not. However, with quantum computers on the horizon we also add an additional categorization, which takes a different approach on long-term security.

Bounded vs unbounded. We distinguish computationally bounded and unbounded adversaries. For the former, we assume that the number of computations the adversary can perform is bounded above by some polynomial in the security parameter. Security is then proved under some computational assumption; that is, breaking the scheme would require the adversary to solve some computational problem which is believed to become super-polynomially more complex when increasing the security parameter. This approach is also taken for most other

S. Krenn and T. Lorünser, *An Introduction to Secret Sharing*,
SpringerBriefs in Information Security and Cryptography,
https://doi.org/10.1007/978-3-031-28161-7_3

cryptographic primitives, such as encryption or signing. Protocols secure against bounded adversaries are also said to provide *conditional* security.

For the case of unbounded adversaries, we do not pose any restrictions whatsoever on the computational power; schemes secure against such attackers are also called to have *information theoretic* or *unconditional security*, and are of key importance when designing long-term private cryptographic systems. This is because security is guaranteed independent of potential future developments in the computational power of the adversary.

Classical vs quantum. Besides the standard definitions, it is also interesting to distinguish between classical adversaries which have no access to quantum resources and quantum adversaries which can use quantum computers or quantum measurement equipment to attack systems. In that sense, quantum adversaries with access to scalable quantum computers are assumed to break asymmetric cryptography relying on number theoretical problems, including a variety of the fundamental assumptions in modern cryptography, e.g., those related to integer factorization including the RSA assumption, or those related to discrete logarithms in finite groups, including elliptic curves. If a protocol can resist quantum adversaries they are called *quantum-safe*. Currently, besides information theoretic cryptography, which does not rely on any complexity assumption at all, many symmetric cryptographic schemes, including many ciphers, hash functions, or message authentication codes (MACs), are considered secure against quantum attacks for appropriately chosen security parameters. Additionally, an entire branch in cryptography called *post-quantum cryptography* (PQC) emerged in over the last decades which aims at developing novel quantum resistant asymmetric cryptography. Post-quantum cryptography relates its hardness on problems which are assumed to be intractable also for quantum computers. Although first PQC schemes are already standardized, the research field is still relatively young and subject to change. However, this topic is only relevant for very few of the protocols presented in the following chapters. Following the paradigm of cryptographic agility, we recommend that recent developments in PQC be examined for possible replacements of non-quantum-safe components and that any implementation be designed in such a way that upgrading of such components is readily possible if needed or possible.

3.2 Network Model

Regarding the network model, we only distinguish two cases:

Synchronous vs asynchronous. In synchronous systems, it is assumed that protocols proceed in rounds: all messages sent in one round are available to their receivers at the beginning of the next round. This assumption often allows for elegant protocols and relatively simple proofs. However, such a network model is only realistic if all nodes run at roughly the same speed, the network is very stable, etc.

In contrast, in an asynchronous model, also network latency or simply different computation speeds on different nodes where one does not want to always wait for the slowest node are modeled. Assuming an asynchronous network is often far closer to reality, in particular for protocols that are to be carried out over the Internet and not only, e.g., in a company-internal data center. However, allowing asynchronicity often causes a considerable overhead in the computational costs of a protocol, and also results in much more intricate security proofs.

3.3 Protocol Level

On a protocol level, there are various properties one has to distinguish when classifying adversaries.

Passive vs active. This is the most basic categorization of adversaries on a protocol level. A passive adversary is only allowed to corrupt a party in the sense that he may see the party's internal state and all messages it receives or sends, but it is not allowed to change the behavior of the machine. Such adversaries are also called *honest-but-curious*. In contrast, an active or *Byzantine* adversary may in general force corrupted nodes to deviate arbitrarily from the protocol specification.

Adaptive vs non-adaptive. Generally speaking, a non-adaptive adversary has to decide which parties to corrupt right away when the protocol starts. On the contrary, an adaptive adversary is allowed to corrupt parties depending on what he has already seen in the protocol so far. That is, an adaptive adversary is allowed to corrupt the "most promising" parties at a given stage of the protocol. As an example, one can think of a non-adaptive adversary as a malicious party which already compromises a system at manufacturing time, but which cannot compromise additional devices once they have been shipped, which would still be able for an adaptive adversary. From a practical point of view, adaptive security clearly becomes more important with an increasing lifetime of the system.

The precise meaning of adaptiveness depends on the concrete protocol and will be specified in detail for each protocol.

Static vs mobile. Assuming a static adversary means that once a party got corrupted, it will stay corrupted until the end of the system. This may be reasonable for short living systems. However, in the case of long-term storage scenarios, a single node might be reset to an honest state once the corruption is detected. We call such an adversary mobile, as he is able to corrupt different nodes at different points in time. Sometimes the respective corruptions are referred to as *transient*. A special case of mobile adversaries are so-called *smash-and-grab* attacks. There, it is assumed that the adversary corrupts a node, copies its entire internal state, and immediately leaves the node again. For instance, this is meaningful when one wants to model data leaks where an insider copies information and makes it publicly available.

Schemes offering protection against mobile adversaries are presented in Chapter 8.

Rushing vs non-rushing. This differentiation is specific to robust secret sharing schemes, cf. Chapter 6, namely when an adversary sends maliciously altered shares back to the user, e.g., in order to make it impossible to reconstruct the shared secret. There, a non-rushing adversary is forced to decide how he wants to alter the shares of corrupted servers before the reconstruction phase starts. A rushing adversary has the additional possibility to first see the shares sent by the honest nodes, and then to decide how to alter the shares.

This adaptive behavior of the adversary must not be confused with the categorization of adaptive or non-adaptive adversaries, which lets the adversary decide which parties to corrupt; so, even an adaptive adversary may be non-rushing or vice versa.

Honest vs corrupted dealer. An honest dealer is always assumed to send consistent shares to all servers, whereas a corrupted dealer might send arbitrary and inconsistent shares to the servers. In particular, for a corrupted dealer it cannot be guaranteed that every qualified set of shares reconstructs to the same secret, or whether it reconstructs to a valid secret at all. While assuming a dishonest dealer might seem artificial at first glance, this might, e.g., happen due to corrupted devices sending altered messages on the network interface without the user noticing. Also, transmission errors on a network level could be detected if a scheme is resistant against dishonest dealers.

Secret sharing protocols that can withstand malicious dealers are called *verifiable*, whereas all others are said to be *non-verifiable*, cf. also Chapter 7.

Chapter 4
Basic Secret Sharing

In this section we formally define the basic concepts of secret sharing schemes, and present some of the most fundamental secret sharing schemes that will also be used as subroutines in some of the subsequent sections.

A secret sharing scheme allows a dealer to distribute a secret s between n parties P_i for $i = 1, \ldots, n$ such that the secret can only be reconstructed if a *qualified subset* of these parties collaborates, while no other (*unqualified*) subset can learn any information about the secret. That is, if the members of a qualified set work together, they will be able to recover the shared information, while no other set of users will be able to do so. The set of all qualified subsets forms the access structure of the system. It is natural to only consider cases where any superset of a qualified set is again qualified, i.e., a set of parties cannot lose their access rights if additional parties join.

Definition 4.1 A set $\Gamma \subseteq 2^{\{1,\ldots,n\}}$ is called a *monotone access structure* on $\{1, \ldots, n\}$ if it is a family of sets such that the following is satisfied: if $\mathcal{A} \in \Gamma$ and $\mathcal{B} \supseteq \mathcal{A}$, then $\mathcal{B} \in \Gamma$. A set $\mathcal{G} \in \Gamma$ is called *qualified*, a set $\mathcal{N} \notin \Gamma$ is called *non-qualified*.

For the sake of simplicity we here identified the set $\mathcal{P} = \{P_1, \ldots, P_n\}$ of parties with the set $\{1, \ldots, n\}$.

Here and in the following, we will mainly focus on threshold schemes, where a set is qualified if it consists of at least k parties for some fixed $k \leq n$. That is, for a threshold scheme, the access structure is given by $\Gamma = \{\mathcal{G} \subseteq \{1, \ldots, n\} : |\mathcal{G}| \geq k\}$.

We can now formally define a secret sharing scheme for an access structure Γ.

Definition 4.2 A *secret sharing scheme* for a set S of secrets and a monotone access structure $\Gamma \subseteq 2^{\{1,\ldots,n\}}$ is a pair of PPT algorithms share, reconstruct:

share: On input $s \in S$, this algorithm outputs shares $\sigma_1, \ldots, \sigma_n \in \{0,1\}^*$.
reconstruct: On input $\{(i, \sigma_i) : i \in \mathcal{G}\}$ this algorithm outputs $s' \in S$ or $\bot$.

The algorithms further satisfy the following security properties:

© The Author(s), under exclusive license to Springer Nature Switzerland AG 2023
S. Krenn and T. Lorünser, *An Introduction to Secret Sharing*,
SpringerBriefs in Information Security and Cryptography,
https://doi.org/10.1007/978-3-031-28161-7_4

Completeness: For every qualified set, reconstruct recovers the original secret s. That is, there exists a negligible function negl such that for all $s \in S$ and all $G \in \Gamma$ we have that:

$$\Pr\left[s = s' : (\sigma_1, \ldots, \sigma_n) \xleftarrow{\$} \text{share}(s),\right.$$
$$\left. s' \xleftarrow{\$} \text{reconstruct}\left(\{(i, \sigma_i) : i \in G\}\right) \right] \geq 1 - \text{negl}(\lambda).$$

Privacy: Any unqualified set of shares does not reveal anything about the original secret s. That is, for every PPT algorithm A there exists a negligible function negl such that for every non-qualified set $N \notin \Gamma$ we have that:

$$\Pr\left[s = s' : (\sigma_1, \ldots, \sigma_n) \xleftarrow{\$} \text{share}(s),\right.$$
$$\left. s' \xleftarrow{\$} \text{A}\left(\{(i, \sigma_i) : i \in N\}\right) \right] \leq \frac{1}{n} + \text{negl}(\lambda).$$

A secret sharing scheme is called *perfectly complete* if negl = 0 in the completeness property. Furthermore, the scheme is *perfectly private*, if no unqualified set of shares leaks any information about the secret in an information theoretic sense, i.e., if negl = 0 in the privacy definition. Otherwise, the scheme is called *computationally private*.

Finally, an important efficiency parameter of secret sharing schemes is the so-called *information rate*, which is defined by ratio of secret message length to the maximum share length generated by the sharing algorithm. In the case of unconditional security it can be shown that the information rate is upper bounded by 1, meaning that the shares are at least as long as the message (and this bound can be achieved for many relevant access structures). However, for computational secure schemes it is even possible to achieve information rates much larger than 1, thus, the messages are longer than the share size, which is very favorable, e.g., for bulk encoding in storage scenarios.

Symbol	Semantics	Restrictions
n	number of parties	
k	threshold required to reconstruct the secret	$k \leq n$
t	maximum number of corrupted participants	$t < k$, typically $k = t + 1$
s	secret to be distributed	typically $s \in \mathbb{Z}_q$
P_i	ith party/server	
σ_i	share given to P_i	

Table 4.1 Overview of notation used in this document.

Table 4.1 gives an overview of the parameters and notation used in this document to describe secret sharing schemes.

4.1 Perfectly Private Secret Sharing

In the following we first introduce a very basic (n, n)-threshold scheme which can be extended to threshold access structures with additional overhead, and then present the broadly used Shamir's scheme for arbitrary thresholds with optimal information rate.

4.1.1 Additive and Replicated Secret Sharing

Additive secret sharing can be considered the most basic form of perfectly secure secret sharing. It is based on the idea that each party holds a random value, however, they sum up to the given secret. The idea is rather simple and informally the security can be compared to one-time-pad in the most basic case with only two parties involved. In that sense, the scheme is also optimal in size but not very flexible, because the access structure only contains the set of all shares, i.e., it is a n-out-of-n secret sharing. The scheme is defined in the following.

Algorithm 4.1: Additive Secret Sharing

share: On input $s \in \mathcal{S} := \mathbb{Z}_q$, this algorithm chooses $a_1, \ldots, a_{n-1} \xleftarrow{\$} \mathbb{Z}_q$ and defines:

$$a_n := s - \sum_{i=1}^{n-1} a_i .$$

The algorithm now outputs $\sigma_i := a_i$ for $i = 1, \ldots, n$.

reconstruct: On input all n shares $(\sigma_1, \ldots, \sigma_n)$, this algorithm computes simply the sum of all shares $s' = \sum_{i=1}^{n} \sigma_i$ in $\mathbb{Z}_q[x]$ and outputs it.

We obtain the following theorem:

Theorem 4.1 *For every q and every n, the above secret sharing scheme is perfectly complete and perfectly private according to Definition 4.2.*

Proof Completeness of this scheme follows immediately by the uniqueness of the sum of shares. To see that the scheme is perfectly private, note that for the sum R_{n-1} of any set of $n-1$ shares and every s', there exists a unique additional share σ_r such that $R + \sigma_r = s'$. □

In summary, the scheme provides unconditional security and is ideal in the sense that it achieves an information rate of 1, i.e., the individual shares have the same size as the secret. Furthermore it is additively homomorphic: Let be given two secrets s_0 and s_1, and corresponding shares $(\sigma_{0,1}, \ldots, \sigma_{0,n})$ and $(\sigma_{1,1}, \ldots, \sigma_{1,n})$, respectively. Now, upon reconstruction of the sums of the shares, i.e., of $(\sigma_1, \ldots, \sigma_n)$

where $\sigma_i = \sigma_{0,i} + \sigma_{1,i}$ for all $i = 1, \ldots, n$, the algorithm will recover the sum of the underlying secrets, i.e., of $s = s_0 + s_1$. However, it provides only very basic functionality and does not give any verifiability or robustness guarantees.

Replicated secret sharing. Additionally, to achieve more flexible access structures, and in particular threshold access structures on the basis of additive secret sharing, replicated secret sharing was introduced. Let therefore $\mathcal{Z}$ denote the set of all maximum unqualified sets, i.e., all sets containing $k - 1$ nodes, such that it consists of $|\mathcal{Z}| = \binom{n}{k-1}$ sets.

On a high level, the algorithm now works as follows. A random value is assigned to each set in $\mathcal{Z}$ and distributed to parties which are not part of the respective set. Similar to additive secret sharing, the random values sum up to the secret s. Thus, parties of any set in $\mathcal{Z}$ or any subset thereof do not have the corresponding value for that set and cannot reconstruct the secret. To the contrary, an admissible set of at least k can reconstruct the secret, because for each set in $\mathcal{Z}$ there exists a party that is not included in that set and has the corresponding random number for that set.

We omit a formal description of the scheme here, as replicated secret sharing is a special case of the additive secret sharing for generic access structures that will be described in detail in Section 5.1. It can directly be derived from its formulation in Algorithm 5.1 by using threshold adversary structures. Furthermore, a significantly more efficient solution for threshold secret sharing will be presented in the following section.

Replicated secret sharing is perfectly secure but produces larger shares and is therefore not optimal in size. However, reconstruction is computationally trivial for typical groups and high threshold values. Sharing as well as reconstruction requires $|\mathcal{Z}|$ additions. Also the storage overhead is lower if the threshold is close to n, or if n in relatively small. The information rate is $1/\binom{n-1}{k-1}$. For $k = n$ the scheme results in the basic additive secret sharing presented above. Replicated secret sharing is also additive homomorph, because it is based additive secret sharing as underlying method. The scheme has no robustness or verifiability whatsoever.

4.1.2 Shamir Secret Sharing

We next recap the perfectly private threshold secret sharing scheme proposed by Shamir [123] allowing for highly efficient implementations in software and hardware [126].

Let therefore be n the number of participants, $k \le n$ be the threshold required for reconstruction, and $q \ge n$ be an arbitrary prime. The scheme is now based on the observation that in a field a polynomial of degree $k - 1$ is uniquely determined by k values, while knowing the function values on at most $k - 1$ positions does not reveal any information about the slope on any position different from the known ones. To share a secret s, the dealer now chooses a random polynomial $f(x)$ of degree $k - 1$ such that $f(0) = s$, and gives $f(i)$ to P_i for $i = 1, \ldots, n$. To reconstruct the secret from sufficiently many shares, the polynomial can be reconstructed, and evaluated at 0.

More formally, the scheme is defined via the following two algorithms:

Algorithm 4.2: Shamir [123]

---

share: On input $s \in \mathcal{S} := \mathbb{Z}_q$, this algorithm chooses $a_1, \ldots, a_{k-1} \stackrel{\$}{\leftarrow} \mathbb{Z}_q$ such that $a_{k-1} \neq 0$, and defines:

$$f(x) := a_{k-1}x^{k-1} + \cdots + a_1x + s.$$

The algorithm now outputs $\sigma_i := f(i)$ for $i = 1, \ldots, n$.

reconstruct: On input at least k inputs of the form (i, σ_i), this algorithm computes the unique interpolation polynomial $g(x)$ of degree $k - 1$ in $\mathbb{Z}_q[x]$, and outputs $s' = g(0)$.

We obtain the following theorem, cf. Shamir [123]:

Theorem 4.2 *For every prime $q > n$, and every k, n with $k \leq n$, the above secret sharing scheme is perfectly complete and perfectly private according to Definition 4.2.*

Proof Completeness of this scheme follows immediately by the uniqueness of the interpolation polynomial. To see that the scheme is perfectly private, note that for any set of $k - 1$ shares and every s', there exists a unique polynomial $g_r(x)$ of degree $k - 1$ such that $g_r(x) = s'$.   □

In summary, the Shamir secret sharing scheme is an unconditionally secure, ideal, and additively homomorphic threshold scheme. Thus, it has an information rate of 1, i.e., shares are as long as the shared secret. The scheme does not provide any robustness or verifiability per se, however, if an error decoding algorithm is used in the reconstruction phase it can be made robust up to a certain level as discussed in Chapter 6. Moreover, an efficient batch verification mechanism based on the homomorphic property has been shown in [53].

4.2 Computationally Private Secret Sharing

In a perfectly private secret sharing scheme each share needs to be at least as large as the secret itself. (More formally, the number of possible shares per party needs to be at least as large as the number of possible secrets to be shared.) Informally, to see this, consider a maximum unqualified set of shares, i.e., a set $\mathcal{N} \notin \Gamma$ such that after adding any further share to $\mathcal{N}$, one obtains a qualified set. Now, as $\mathcal{N}$ did not contain any information about the shared secret, all information about the secret is added when adding this one additional share, which thus has to be as large as the secret itself. Schemes achieving this bound are called *ideal*. However, this means that even for ideal schemes the storage overhead is the same as when storing n replicas of the original data. This is significantly worse than in non-private information dispersal systems [112] or in common RAID systems, where the overhead is only about n/k if the system should be able to compensate for up to $n - k$ losses.

Krawczyk [93] proposed a system to combine the space efficiency of information dispersal with the privacy of secret sharing schemes, if one is willing to restrict the class of adversaries to PPT algorithms. That is, the proposed scheme is secure as long as the computational power of any hypothetical adversary is bounded above by a polynomial.

On a high level, the idea is to first encrypt the data m using a symmetric encryption scheme, and then apply the secret sharing scheme to the used key and the information dispersal scheme to the resulting ciphertext.

More formally, the algorithms share and reconstruct are as follows, where (Enc, Dec) is a symmetric key encryption scheme, (share′, reconstruct′) is a perfectly private secret sharing scheme such as the one presented in Section 4.1.2, and (share″, reconstruct″) is an information dispersal scheme:

Algorithm 4.3: Krawczyk [93]

share: On input data s, this algorithm first draws a random encryption key K for the symmetric encryption scheme, and computes $e = \mathsf{Enc}_K(s)$. It then computes:

$$(\sigma_{K,1}, \ldots, \sigma_{K,n}) \xleftarrow{s} \mathsf{share}'(K) \quad \text{and} \quad (\sigma_{e,1}, \ldots, \sigma_{e,n}) \xleftarrow{s} \mathsf{share}''(e).$$

The algorithm outputs $\sigma_i = (\sigma_{K,i}, \sigma_{e,i})$ for $i = 1, \ldots, n$.

reconstruct: On input at least k shares of the form $(i, \sigma_i) = (i, (\sigma_{K,i}, \sigma_{e,i}))$, this algorithm first computes:

$$K' \xleftarrow{s} \mathsf{reconstruct}'(\{(i, \sigma_{K,i}) : i \in \mathcal{I}\}) \quad \text{and}$$

$$e' \xleftarrow{s} \mathsf{reconstruct}''(\{(i, \sigma_{e,i}) : i \in \mathcal{I}\}),$$

where $\mathcal{I}$ is the set of input indices. It then outputs $s' \xleftarrow{s} \mathsf{Dec}_K(e')$, or $s' := \perp$ if one of K', e' was equal to $\perp$.

It is easy to see that for long secrets s, the size of the shares is dominated by that from the information dispersal scheme. Similar to Shamir's scheme, a simple and efficient scheme to disperse k elements $a_0, \ldots, a_{k-1} \in \mathbb{Z}_q$ is to define the polynomial $f(x) = a_{k-1}x^{k-1} + \cdots + a_1 x + a_0$, and to output shares $\sigma_i = f(i)$ for $i = 1, \ldots, n$. Now, if the encryption scheme maps into $\mathbb{Z}_q$, this information dispersal scheme – and as a result also Krawzcyk's computationally secure secret sharing scheme – asymptotically achieves the optimal storage overhead of n/k.

We want to stress that IND-CPA security introduced in Definition 2.5 is not necessary, but the weaker security requirements of *one-query indistinguishability* and *one-query key-unrecoverability* would already be sufficient for the construction to be sound, cf. Rogaway and Bellare [114]. However, we defined IND-CPA security as it is achieved by virtually all practically relevant symmetric encryption schemes anyways.

To recap, the above scheme provides computational security, relying on the security of the selected encryption scheme. It achieves an information rate of about $k \geq 1$. It is easy to see that the scheme does not offer any homomorphic properties. Finally, it does not provide any robustness or verifiability per se, however, already in the original work was an extension presented to make it robust, which is discussed in Chapter 6.

4.3 Ramp Secret Sharing

While the scheme presented in Section 4.1.2 offers unconditional security, it requires each share to be as large as the secret value itself. On the other hand, the scheme from Section 4.2 minimizes the size of the shares at the costs of computational security.

A possible trade-off between small share sizes and unconditional security is offered by *ramp secret sharing* schemes [17, 137]. In such schemes, sets of shares can no longer only be qualified and non-qualified; rather, there are also intermediate sets which are insufficient to recover the secret, but which may leak partial information about the shared secret.

In the case of threshold secret sharing schemes, this results in the following security guarantees for a (k, l, n) ramp threshold secret sharing scheme. On the one hand, the secret can be efficiently recovered from any set of at least k shares. On the other hand, no information about the secret — in an information theoretic sense — can be obtained from any set of at most $k - l$ shares. For the case of $k - l + j$ shares for $1 \leq j < l$, the scheme guarantees that at most $j/l \cdot H(S)$ is disclosed, where $H(S)$ denotes the entropy of the random variable corresponding to the secret s.

The ramp version of Shamir secret sharing is a generalization of the standard scheme, which introduces a configurable amount of data words l that are packed into the Shamir algorithm. More specifically, the original scheme from Section 4.1.2 can only encode one secret element per sharing polynomial which leads to the low information rate of 1. By packing more than a single secret into one polynomial the information rate can be increased. That is, instead of encoding a single $s \in \mathbb{Z}_q$ as the constant term of the polynomial, a vector $s = (s_0, \ldots, s_{l-1}) \in \mathbb{Z}_q^l$ now defines the coefficients of the l low-order terms. Having access to k shares enables to recompute the polynomial and hence the entire secret vector; on the other hand, only having at most $k - l$ shares does not give any information about s, by a similar argument as in the original Shamir scheme.

In detail, the scheme by the following algorithm.

Algorithm 4.4: Shamir ramp secret sharing

share: On input $s = (s_0, \ldots, s_{l-1}) \in \mathcal{S} := \mathbb{Z}_q^l$, this algorithm chooses $k - l$ random

coefficients $a_l, \ldots, a_{k-1} \xleftarrow{\$} \mathbb{Z}_q$ such that $a_{k-1} \neq 0$, and defines:

$$f(x) := a_{k-1}x^{k-1} + \cdots + a_l x^l + s_{l-1}x^{l-1} + \cdots + s_1 x + s_0 .$$

The algorithm now outputs $\sigma_i := f(i)$ for $i = 1, \ldots, n$.

reconstruct: On input at least k inputs of the form (i, σ_i), this algorithm computes
   the unique interpolation polynomial

$$g(x) = a'_{k-1}x^{k-1} + \cdots + a'_l x^l + s'_{l-1}x^{l-1} + \cdots + s'_1 x + s'_0$$

of degree $k - 1$ in $\mathbb{Z}_q[x]$, and outputs $s' = (s'_0, \ldots, s'_{l-1})$.

In summary, the above ramp secret sharing scheme achieves unconditional privacy against $k - l$ colluding shares at an information rate of l. It inherits the additively homomorphic properties from the Shamir secret sharing scheme. No verifiability or robustness guarantees are given.

However, as pointed out by Iwamoto and Yamamoto [84], the above scheme does not imply *strong* security for a ramp scheme. That is, while no intermediate set can reconstruct more than a fraction of j/l of the secret, it may be possible that it fully learns certain components of the secret, while not learning anything about the others, see [84] for an example. For schemes that provide such strong security guarantees in the sense that no intermediate set may learn individual components of the secret explicitly, as well as schemes for arbitrary types of access structures, we refer the interested reader to the original literature [59, 60, 84].

Chapter 5
Beyond Threshold Access Structures

Before presenting secret sharing schemes in more advanced adversary models, we next give a short overview of more complex access structures than simple threshold access structures. We therefore first present a scheme for arbitrary access structures in Section 5.1, and then give an introduction to compartmented secret sharing schemes in Section 5.2. Finally, we will give an overview over so-called hierarchical access structures in Section 5.3. In particular for the latter we will keep the discussion on a rather informal level, as we believe that for a distributed storage system, threshold (and possibly compartmented) schemes reflect the most realistic trust models.

5.1 Additive Secret Sharing for Generic Access Structures

This scheme is the generalization of additive and replicated secrets sharing to allow for generic access structures. However, to better describe this scheme we use the idea of an adversary structure which can be considered the complimentary view of an access structure. An adversary structure is defined by the set of all maximal coalitions of participants which are not able to recover the secret.

Let $\mathcal{Z}$ be an adversary structure that contains m subsets of the numbers $1, \ldots, n$ of variable size representing groups of colluding parties. The algorithm works by assigning a random number to each adversary set and distributing them in a way such that each adversary set of colluding parties has not all information required to reconstruct the secret. Let the elements of $\mathcal{Z}$ be labeled Z_j, $j = 1, 2, \ldots, m$. During the sharing, uniformly random values are assigned to the adversary sets, $r_{Z_1}, \ldots, r_{Z_{m-1}}$ with $r_{Z_m} = s - (r_{Z_1} + \cdots + r_{Z_{m-s}})$. Share σ_i then consists of all the r values whose indices do not contain the value i, where $i = 1, 2, \ldots, n$

Algorithm 5.1: Additive Secret Sharing for Generic Access Structure

share: On input $s \in S := \mathbb{Z}_q$ and adversary structure $\mathcal{Z} = \{Z_1, \ldots, Z_m \mid Z_j \subset \{1, \ldots, n\}\}$ this algorithm chooses $r_{Z_1}, \ldots, r_{Z_{m-1}} \xleftarrow{\$} \mathbb{Z}_q$ and defines:

© The Author(s), under exclusive license to Springer Nature Switzerland AG 2023
S. Krenn and T. Lorünser, *An Introduction to Secret Sharing*,
SpringerBriefs in Information Security and Cryptography,
https://doi.org/10.1007/978-3-031-28161-7_5

$$r_{Z_m} := s - \sum_{i=1}^{m-1} r_{Z_i} .$$

The algorithm now outputs $\sigma_i := \{r_{Z_j} \mid i \notin Z_j\}$ for all shares $i = 1, \ldots, n$.

reconstruct: On input shares $\{\sigma_i \mid i \in K\}$, such that for all Z_j from $1 \leq j \leq m$ there
    exists $i_{Z_j} \in K$ such that $i_{Z_j} \notin Z_i$, this algorithm recovers the secret by summing
    up all random components contributed by each adversary set as follows:

$$s' = \sum_{i=1}^{m} r_{Z_i}$$

in $\mathbb{Z}_q[x]$ and outputs it.

We obtain the following theorem:

Theorem 5.1 *For every q, every n, and every adversary structure $\mathcal{Z}$, the above
secret sharing scheme is perfectly complete and perfectly private according to Definition 4.2.*

Proof Completeness of this scheme follows immediately by the uniqueness of the
sum of shares and the fact that all nodes which are not part of an adversary set
contribute random values to restore the secret. This ensures, that all admissible sets of
nodes always comprise a full set of random values r_{Z_i} for $i = 1, \ldots, m$ corresponding
to the sets of the adversary structure. To see that the scheme is perfectly private, note
that for each set in the adversary structure there exists a uniformly random value
which is not known to them, i.e., they have no knowledge on the final secret. Thus,
every admissible set of shares always contains at least one node not in the adversary
set Z_i for each set of the adversary structure $\mathcal{Z}$.   □

To recap, the scheme offers unconditional security. The generality of support-
ing arbitrary access structures comes at the price of a low information rate of
$1/\max_{1 \leq i \leq n} |\{r_Z \mid i \notin Z \in \mathcal{Z}\}|$. The scheme is additively homomorphic due to the
homomorphic property of the underlying additive secret sharing scheme. Finally, no
guarantees regarding verifiability or robustness are given.

5.2 Compartmented Secret Sharing

So far, we assumed that an arbitrary choice of k out of n servers should be sufficient
to reconstruct the distributed secret. However, to further increase security, it might
be imaginable that no set of servers under the legislation of the same country should
be able to reconstruct the secret. This could be modeled by using a *compartmented
threshold access structure*. In such a scheme, one could for instance require that at

least two out of four servers located in country A, *and* at least two out of three servers located in country B have to contribute to the reconstruction. Thus, even if all servers located in country A would be compromised due to a changing legal environment, it would be impossible for them to reconstruct the secret – even though the overall threshold of the scheme is four, and thus sufficiently many servers would have been located in this country.

More formally, in a compartmented threshold secret sharing scheme the set of parties $\mathcal{P}$ is divided into m disjoint subsets $\mathcal{P}_1, \ldots, \mathcal{P}_m$, i.e., $\mathcal{P} = \bigcup_{i=1}^{m} \mathcal{P}_i$ and $\mathcal{P}_i \cap \mathcal{P}_j = \emptyset$ for all $i \neq j$. Let furthermore $n_i := |\mathcal{P}_i|$ and k_i be the threshold required for $\mathcal{P}_i$, for all $i = 1, \ldots, m$. The respective access structure is then given by:

$$\Gamma := \{\mathcal{G} \subseteq \mathcal{P} : |\mathcal{G} \cap \mathcal{P}_i| \geq k_i \text{ for all } i = 1, \ldots, m\} .$$

Schemes for such access structures were first proposed by Simmons [125] and Brickell [30]. In the following we will describe the scheme due to Ghodosi et al. [73].

On a high level, a secret sharing scheme for such an access structure can be obtained by first decomposing the secret into m shares, which are then again shared using a (n_i, k_i) threshold scheme, cf. also Figure 5.1 for a high-level visualization of the reconstruction process.

In the following description, let $(\text{share}_i', \text{reconstruct}_i')$ refer to a (n_i, k_i) threshold scheme, potentially those from Algorithms 4.2 and 4.3. Furthermore, for notational convenience, let $\mathcal{P}_i := \{P_{i,1}, \ldots, P_{i,n_i}\}$ for all i.

Algorithm 5.2: Ghodosi et al. [73]

share: On input a secret $s \in \mathbb{Z}_q$, this algorithm proceeds in two steps:

1. First, it chooses $s_1, \ldots, s_{m-1} \xleftarrow{\$} \mathbb{Z}_q$ and set $s_m := s - \sum_{i=1}^{m-1} s_i$.
2. For each $i = 1, \ldots, m$, define $(\sigma_{i,1}, \ldots, \sigma_{i,n_i}) \xleftarrow{\$} \text{share}_i'(s_i)$.

The algorithm outputs $\sigma_{i,j}$ to $P_{i,j}$.

reconstruct: Given sufficiently many shares $\sigma_{i,j}$ as inputs, the algorithm recomputes

$$s_i' \xleftarrow{\$} \text{reconstruct}_i'(\{(j, \sigma_{i,j}) : i \in \mathcal{P}_j\}) \text{ for all } i = 1, \ldots, m .$$

It outputs $s' = \sum_{i=1}^{m} s_i'$.

The proof of the following theorem can be found in the original literature [73].

Theorem 5.2 *If all* $(\text{share}_i', \text{reconstruct}_i')$ *are perfectly private threshold sharing schemes, the above scheme is a perfectly private compartmented threshold secret sharing scheme if* $q > \max_{1 \leq i \leq m} n_i$ *is prime. If all schemes are computationally private, the resulting scheme is computationally private.*

In summary, Ghodosi et al.'s scheme achieves unconditional security if the scheme deployed as building block does so; if the building block only provides computational

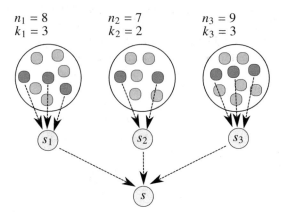

Fig. 5.1 Example for the Ghodosi et al. [73] compartmented access structure and reconstruction

security, then this is also the case for the resulting scheme. Similarly, the scheme inherits any homomorphic properties from its building block. Furthermore, the achieved information rate equals the minimum information rate that is achieved for the individual $\mathcal{P}_i$. No verifiability or robustness guarantees are given. In particular, when using the scheme from Section 4.1.2, the scheme is unconditionally secure, additively homomorphic, and achieves an information rate equals of 1; when using the scheme from Section 4.2, conditional security without homomorphic properties, but an information rate of $\min_{1 \leq i \leq m} k_i$ is achieved.

We want to stress that Ghodosi et al. [73] further refined their scheme, such that an additional threshold on the overall number of shares can be required. That is, their scheme allows one to realize access structures of the form:

$$\Gamma := \{\mathcal{G} \subseteq \mathcal{P} : |\mathcal{G} \cap \mathcal{P}_i| \geq k_i \text{ for all } i = 1, \ldots, m \quad \wedge \quad |\mathcal{G} \cap \mathcal{P}| \geq k\} \, ,$$

for an arbitrary integer k satisfying $\sum_{i=1}^{m} k_i \leq k \leq n$.

Furthermore, other variants can be realized in a straightforward manner. For instance, one could require that only sufficiently many shares from a certain number k of compartments need to be available in order to reconstruct the secret. In this case, Step (1) of Algorithm 5.2 would decompose s into $s_1, \ldots, s_m$ using an (m, k) threshold secret sharing scheme.

5.3 Hierarchical Secret Sharing

In all access structures considered so far we did not distinguish between different types of parties. However, this might become necessary in certain situations. For instance, the president of a company should have more rights than his vice-presidents. In the most basic version, such differing rights could be realized by simply giving a different number of shares to the different types of parties [123]. More fine grained rights can be assigned using so-called *hierarchical secret sharing schemes*, first suggest by Simmons [125], which we will informally discuss in the following.

5.3.1 Defining Thresholds on Different Levels

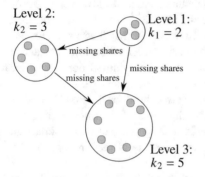 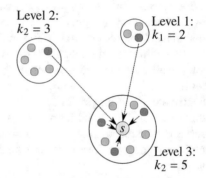

Fig. 5.2 Simmons' hierarchical access structure.

Fig. 5.3 An example of subset of shares able to reconstruct the secret.

Simmons [125] suggested a setting where participants are divided into disjoint levels. This is an interesting variety that allows to map secret sharing to the hierarchical structure of companies managing several employees with different competences. In this setup, each level i contains n_i participants and is associated to a different threshold k_i. This means that subsets of participants can reconstruct the secret at any level i, provided that the number of participants from level i is greater or equal to k_i. In the case that not enough participants from a certain level are present, the missing ones can be replaced by members of any higher level, cf. Figure 5.2. Letting $\mathcal{P} = \bigcup_{i=1}^{l} \mathcal{P}_i$ for disjoint $\mathcal{P}_1, \ldots, \mathcal{P}_l$, the access structure to be realized is given by:

$$\Gamma := \left\{ G \subseteq \mathcal{P} : \exists i : \left| G \cap \bigcup_{j=1}^{i} \mathcal{P}_j \right| \geq k_i \right\}$$

For example, if two participants on the third level are not available, their shares can be replaced by two participants of the second level, two participants from the first level, or one participant from the first level and one participant from the second level respectively, see Figure 5.3; alternative qualified sets in this example would have included two shares from level 2 plus one share from level 1, or simply two shares from level 1.

Simmons' hierarchy allows one to make decisions even in the absence of some persons in authority. Simmons called this hierarchical access structure *multilevel secret sharing*, but often in literature "hierarchical" and "multilevel" are used synonymously. For this hierarchical framework, Brickell [30] proposed two ideal secret sharing schemes that are ideal. Later, Ghodosi presents in [73] a more efficient ideal secret sharing scheme, which is also perfectly private.

5.3.2 Enforcing Participants from Higher Levels

While in Simmons' hierarchy model participants from lower levels can be replaced by participants from higher levels, Tassa et al. [129, 130] consider a slightly different hierarchical access structure. The main difference is that Tassa's secret sharing scheme addresses situations where even though participants on higher and lower levels can contribute to reconstruct the secret, still a minimal number of higher-level participants is required. In their approach participants from different levels contribute. For example, let us assume that the threshold for the first level is k_1, the threshold for the second level is k_2, and the threshold of the third level is k_3. The secret can be reconstructed if and only if at least k_3 participants collaborate, and k_2 of them belongs to the second and the first level, and k_1 of them belongs to the first level.

In the context of a distributed storage scenario this approach could be used as follows: one could define in-house data centers to be on the highest level, self-hosted data centers on the second level, and external data centers to be on the third level. One could then require that at least one internal, and another self-hosted data center contribute to the reconstruction. In this way it could be guaranteed that no confidential data is leaked even if all externally hosted data centers collaborate, while one could still profit from higher availability guarantees, e.g., in the case that one out of two in-house storage servers fails.

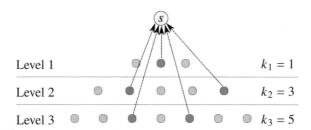

Fig. 5.4 Example of Tassa's hierarchical access structure.

More formally, let $k_1 \leq k_2 \leq \cdots \leq k_l$ be integers specifying the thresholds for levels $1, \ldots, l$. Let furthermore be $\mathcal{P} = \bigcup_{i=1}^{l} \mathcal{P}_i$ (with $\mathcal{P}_i \cap \mathcal{P}_j = \emptyset$ for all $i \neq j$), where for all i, $\mathcal{P}_i$ is the set of parties from level i. Then the access structure for Tassa's hierarchical secret sharing scheme is given by:

$$\Gamma := \left\{ \mathcal{G} \subseteq \mathcal{P} : \left| \mathcal{G} \cap \bigcup_{j=1}^{i} \mathcal{P}_j \right| \geq k_i \text{ for all } i = 1, \ldots, l \right\}. \tag{5.1}$$

See Figure 5.4 for an example with $(k_1, k_2, k_3) = (1, 3, 5)$. There, having 3 shares from the first, and 2 shares from the second level would also have been sufficient to reconstruct the secret, while having all 7 shares from the third level and all 5 shares from the second level would not have been sufficient.

In the following we describe Tassa's algorithm, which can be seen to reduce to Algorithm 4.2 in the special case that $l = 1$. For notational convenience, let $k := k_l$.

Algorithm 5.3: Tassa [129]

---

share: To share a secret $s \in \mathbb{Z}_q$, the dealer proceeds as follows:

1. First, it chooses $a_1, \ldots, a_{k-1} \overset{s}{\leftarrow} \mathbb{Z}_q$ such that $a_{k-1} \neq 0$ and defines:

$$f(x) := a_{k-1} x^{k-1} + \cdots + a_1 x + s.$$

2. For each party P_i the dealer determines j such that $P_i \in \mathcal{P}_j$. It then computes $\sigma_i := f^{(k_{j-1})}(i)$, where $k_0 = 0$. That is, the share for P_i is the $(k_{j-1})^{\text{th}}$ derivative of $f(x)$ at position $x = i$.

Finally, the algorithm outputs $(\sigma_1, \ldots, \sigma_n)$.

reconstruct: Given as input a set of shares $(\{(i, \sigma_i) : i \in \mathcal{I}\})$ such that $|\mathcal{I} \cap \bigcup_{j=1}^{i} \mathcal{P}_j| \geq k_i$ for all $i = 1, \ldots, l$, this algorithm computes the interpolation polynomial $f(x)$ satisfying $\sigma_i = f^{(k_{j-1})}(i)$ for all $i \in |\mathcal{I} \cap \mathcal{P}_j|$. This can be done efficiently using Birkhoff interpolation [13].
It then outputs $s' = f(0)$.

To get an intuition of the functioning of the scheme, consider a "minimal" qualified set $\mathcal{I}$ of users in the sense that $\mathcal{I}$ only contains a minimum number of participants required for each level, i.e., $|\mathcal{I} \cap \bigcup_{j=1}^{i} \mathcal{P}_j| = k_i$ for all $i = 1, \ldots, l$. Then, by interpolating the shares from level l yields the polynomial $f^{(k_{l-1})}(x)$: this is a polynomial of degree $k - 1 - k_{l-1} = k_l - k_{l-1} - 1$, which can be reconstructed from the $k_l - k_{l-1}$ shares from level l. Now, integrating $f^{(k_{l-1})}(x)$ repeatedly $k_{l-1} - k_{l-2}$ times yields a polynomial with $k_{l-1} - k_{l-2}$ unknown coefficients, which can be computed using the $k_{l-1} - k_{l-2}$ shares from level $l - 1$; the resulting polynomial is clearly equal to $f^{(k_{l-2})}(x)$. Iterating over the levels finally yields $f^{(0)}(x) = f(x)$.

On the other hand, of course, having shares of an unqualified set does not reveal any information about the secret, as this would at most allow one to compute a derivative of $f(x)$, which does not contain any information about s.

Formally, the following theorem can be shown [129]:

Theorem 5.3 *For all $k_1 \leq \cdots \leq k_l = k$, all integers n, and all prime numbers q satisfying:*

$$2^{-k+2} \cdot (k-1)^{(k-1)/2} \cdot (k-1)! \cdot n^{(k-1)(k-2)/2} < q , \tag{5.2}$$

the above scheme is a perfectly complete and perfectly private hierarchical secret sharing scheme for (5.1).

We note that the above condition is only required to prove the completeness of the scheme. This is because otherwise the uniqueness of the recovered interpolation polynomial cannot be guaranteed for arbitrary qualified sets.

On the one hand, when using a q of bit-length 64, the condition from Theorem 5.3 can only be satisfied for $k < 8$; for $|q| = 128$ we get $k < 10$, for $|q| = 256$ we get $k < 13$, and for $|q| = 512$ we get $k < 17$. On the other hand, for $|q| \geq 128$ and $k = 5$, this condition is satisfied for n up to at least 10^6, such that the practical limitations of (5.2) will be satisfied in a broad range of relevant scenarios.

5.3.3 Other Hierarchical Access Structures

While in Tassa's approach participants from higher levels can contribute with participants from lower levels, Naskar et al. [103] address the case where such a cooperation is mandatory. This solution is used in scenarios where, for instance, not only the employees should be unable to reconstruct the secret without the president, but also vice versa, e.g., to ensure that labor representatives are present upon access of certain data.

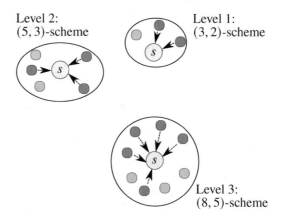

Fig. 5.5 Example of Kothari's hierarchical access structure.

Another hierarchical structure is proposed by Kothari in [91]. Contrary to all other approaches only participants of the same level can contribute to reconstruct the secret. More precisely, in his scenario a separate (k_i, n_i) threshold scheme is associated to each level i of a multilevel group of participants. Thus, it is not possible to cope with concurrency among different hierarchical levels. So when, say, only $s_i < k_i$ participants from level i contribute, then the other $k_i - s_i$ participants cannot be taken from lower or higher levels and the secret cannot be reconstructed. See Figure 5.5 for an example where $(n_1, k_1) = (3, 2)$, $(n_2, k_2) = (5, 3)$, and $(n_3, k_3) = (8, 5)$.

Furthermore, other secret sharing protocols with hierarchical access structures have been proposed that provide additional properties. Chang et al. [40] discuss a scheme where so-called admission tickets are used in order to delegate the capability to reconstruct the secret from high-level participants to lower-level ones. Tentu et al. [131] present an ideal and perfect hierarchical secret sharing scheme that is built on linear codes. Runhua et al. [116] present a secret sharing scheme for the Tassa's hierarchical structure where multiple secrets rather than one can be shared. Kasper et al. [87] show how multiplication can be performed directly on the shares. Further work on hierarchical secret sharing includes verifiable hierarchical secret sharing [133] (cf. also Chapter 7), achieving fairness in hierarchical secret sharing through the use of smart blockchains [138], Finally, Ballico et al. [3] employ hierarchical secret sharing for ad hoc networks.

Due to the different hierarchical secret sharing schemes, Farras et al. [61] formalized the notion of hierarchical access structures. According to this definition an access structure is hierarchical if for any two participants, one of them is hierarchically superior (or equal) to the other one. In particular, if a participant in a subset that is qualified to reconstruct the secret is replaced by another one that is hierarchically superior, then the subset remains qualified. However, according to such definition, approaches where also participants of a lower level, e.g. Naskar's approach [103], are needed to reconstruct the secret or only participants of the same level can contribute, such as Kothari's approach [91], are not part of this class. Finally, e.g., Ito et al. [83] and Charnes et al. [41] introduced additional types of access structures allowing for additional rules, e.g. that a particular set of participants cannot reconstruct the secret or even that one particular participant is allowed to.

Chapter 6
Robust Secret Sharing

Basic secret sharing schemes as discussed in Chapter 4 assume that all parties are honest-but-curious. That is, they are secure as long as at most $k-1$ parties pool their shares, but it is assumed that they otherwise stick to the protocol specification. This modelling however does not consider the case where an adversary sends malicious responses at reconstruction time. Such malicious shares could prevent the reconstruction of the original secret s, or result in a reconstructed secret $s' \neq s$ without the dealer being able to detect this. Unfortunately, basic secret sharing schemes in general do not offer any protection against such misbehavior; schemes offering this level of security are referred to as *robust*. More specifically, in a robust secret sharing scheme, it is guaranteed that given all n shares, of which at most t may have been maliciously modified by an adversary, reconstruction will still result in the original secret s. Robust secret sharing schemes thus do not only protect the confidentiality, but also the integrity of a shared secret.

Now, the adversary model considered in this section is the following: the adversary is fully inactive during the sharing phase of the scheme. After this phase, it may corrupt up to t parties inside $\{P_1, \ldots, P_n\}$. During this corruption process, we consider two subcases: If the adversary specifies all parties to corrupt at a time, i.e., before seeing any information, the adversary is called *non-adaptive*; alternatively, the adversary may specify one party to corrupt at a time, and then decide which party to corrupt next. Such an adversary is called *adaptive*. Here, corruption means that the adversary learns the share of the party, and after that takes over full control of the party.

Now, during the reconstruction phase, the adversary gets to see all communication between the reconstructing user and all honest parties. In every communication round, the adversary can decide for every corrupted party which data is sent to the user, depending on all information it has seen so far. We again distinguish two types of adversaries in this section: *rushing* and *non-rushing* adversaries. A rushing adversary may choose all values to be sent to the adversary after having seen what honest parties sent in previous and the current rounds. A non-rushing adversary has to select all corrupted shares before the reconstruct protocol starts. An adaptive

S. Krenn and T. Lorünser, *An Introduction to Secret Sharing*,
SpringerBriefs in Information Security and Cryptography,
https://doi.org/10.1007/978-3-031-28161-7_6

adversary may further corrupt additional parties after each communication round, as long as no more than t parties get corrupted.

Definition 6.1 A secret sharing scheme according to Definition 4.2 is (t, δ)-*robust*, if it additionally satisfies the following property:

Reconstructability: Given all n shares as input, the output of reconstruct is equal to the original secret with probability at least $1 - \delta$, even if up to t shares were maliciously changed by the adversary.

It can be shown that Shamir's secret sharing scheme is robust for every $t < n/3$. Furthermore, for a meaningful definition in a threshold setting, only $t < k$ needs to be considered for confidentiality reasons. It is thus easy to see that robust secret sharing for $t \geq n/2$ cannot be achieved. In the remainder of this section we will thus focus on the case where $n/3 \leq t < n/2$, and on the case where $k = t + 1$.

Before going into the details of some concrete constructions, we want to mention some straightforward options to construct robust secret sharing schemes. One possibility is to modify Shamir's scheme (cf. Algorithm 4.2) such that the coefficients of the polynomial are chosen from a much larger space than the secret itself, as suggested by Tompa and Woll [132]. In their scheme, one chooses $f(x) \xleftarrow{\$} \mathbb{Z}_{q'}[x]$ such that $f(0) = s$, where $0 \leq s < q$ for some $q \ll q'$. In this way, if computing the interpolation polynomial from modified shares, the constant term of the resulting polynomial would, with high probability, be larger than q. The reconstruction algorithm now searches for a set of shares such that the resulting secret is less than q.

More generally, one could always add error checking mechanisms to plain secret sharing schemes in order to make them robust. For instance, one can add checksums or apply an error-correcting code to the secret s before sharing it using a plain secret sharing scheme. The reconstruction algorithm would now again search for a set of shares such that the resulting secret is correct with respect to those checksums. Given that the size of secrets is often relatively small, e.g., to allow for hardware optimizations, such checksums or error correcting capabilities could also be added on a cross-secret level if certain secrets (e.g., belonging to the same block of a file) will always be recovered jointly.

An unconditionally secure representative of this approach was also pointed out by Cramer, Damgard and Fehr [48]. In this scheme the dealer uses Shamir secret sharing to share all three values, the actual secret $s \in \mathbb{F}$, a random value $r \in \mathbb{F}$, and its product $p = s \cdot r$ together as RSS shares. During reconstruction, a combination of shares is only accepted if the respective values s', r', p' reconstructed also fulfill $p' = r' \cdot s'$. It is easy to see, that this gives an efficient RSS. If $t + 1$ shares are accepted the result must be correct and non of the t corrupt shares can lead to any acceptance except for negligible probability.

Unfortunately, for all approaches of this type, in the worst case all possible qualified sets of shares have to be combined until a valid secret can be reconstructed, resulting in an exponential worst-case performance for any $t = O(n)$. They all follow a basic pattern, i.e., they basically convert a generic secret sharing scheme into one which can detect errors, which subsequently can be converted into a robust secret sharing scheme [95]. Therefore, while naive solutions may be an adequate solution for a small number of parties and/or a relatively small number of corrupted participants —potentially bounded by a constant— these solutions do not scale for larger values of n and t, such that more tailored protocols have to be developed to avoid the exponential worst-case performance.

6.1 Unconditionally Secure Solutions

In the following we describe an unconditionally private RSS schemes, which is based on the idea of Rabin and Ben-Or [113] often referenced as *information checking*. On a high level, in their scheme the dealer extends the share sent to a party by message authentication codes. That is, for every party P_j, the share of P_i is authenticated with a tag $\tau_{i,j}$, and the corresponding key is given to P_j. At reconstruction phase, the shares can now be checked for correctness by checking whether they are accepted by sufficiently many tags. To have a failure probability negligible in λ, MACs with length at least λ bits need to be used, and thus each party needs to additionally store $\Omega(\lambda n)$ bits.

The following scheme was proposed by Cevallos et al. [38], who obtain high security guarantees even though only using weak MACs with short keys and tags. The storage overhead per node is only $\tilde{O}(\lambda + n)$.

Algorithm 6.1: Cevallos et al. [38]

share: On input $s \in \mathbb{Z}_q$, this algorithm executes Shamir's secret sharing scheme to obtain σ_i' for $i = 1, \dots, n$. It then chooses a random key $K_{i,j}$ from the key space of the used MAC scheme for all $i, j = 1, \dots, n$. The algorithm computes

$$\tau_{i,j} \xleftarrow{\$} \mathsf{Mac}_{K_{j,i}}(\sigma_i') \quad \text{for all} \quad i, j = 1, \dots, n.$$

For all $i = 1, \dots, n$, the algorithm sets

$$\sigma_i := (\sigma_i', \tau_{i,1}, \dots, \tau_{i,n}, K_{i,1}, \dots, K_{i,n}),$$

and finally outputs $(\sigma_1, \dots, \sigma_n)$.

reconstruct: Upon receiving inputs $(\sigma_1, \dots, \sigma_n)$ of the above form, this algorithm proceeds in three steps:

   1. For every $i, j = 1, \dots, n$, the algorithms defines $v_{i,j} = 1$ if and only if σ_i' is accepted by the key of P_j, i.e.:

$$v_{i,j} := \begin{cases} 1 & \text{if } \tau_{i,j} = \mathsf{Mac}_{K_{j,i}}(\sigma_i'), \\ 0 & \text{else.} \end{cases}$$

2. The algorithm next computes the largest set I of indices satisfying:

$$\forall i \in I : |\{j \in I : v_{i,j} = 1\}| = \sum_{j \in I} v_{i,j} \geq t + 1 .$$

That is, every σ'_i for $i \in I$ is accepted by at least $t + 1$ parties in I. In particular, all the indices of all honest parties are in I.

3. Using, e.g., the Berlekamp-Welch algorithm [135], the algorithm now computes a polynomial $f(x) \in \mathbb{Z}_q[x]$ of degree $k - 1$ such that $f(i) = \sigma'_i$ for at least $t + 1 + \frac{|I| - (t+1)}{2}$ parties in I. If no such polynomial exists, the algorithm outputs $\perp$, otherwise it returns $s' = f(0)$.

It can now be shown that the above scheme is a secure robust threshold secret sharing scheme. For a proof, we refer to the original literature [38].

Theorem 6.1 *For any positive integer t, any prime $q > n = 2t + 1$, and any ε secure message authentication code with message space $\mathbb{Z}_q$ and $\varepsilon \leq 1/(t + 1)$, the above scheme is an (t, δ)-robust secret sharing scheme for the message space $\mathbb{Z}_q$, with:*

$$\delta \leq e \cdot ((t + 1)\varepsilon)^{(t+1)/2} ,$$

where $e = \exp(1)$.

It is important to note that from the theorem it follows that δ is not only of order ε, but actually of order $\varepsilon^{\Omega(n)}$ for the case that $n = 2t + 1$, allowing for relatively short keys and tags [38]. Table 6.1 provides an overview of the achieved values for δ for different values of t and ε.

		Threshold t of corrupt participants				
		1	2	3	4	5
Security parameter ε	2^{-5}	2^{-2}	2^{-3}	2^{-4}	2^{-5}	2^{-5}
	2^{-10}	2^{-7}	2^{-11}	2^{-14}	2^{-17}	2^{-20}
	2^{-15}	2^{-12}	2^{-18}	2^{-24}	2^{-30}	2^{-35}
	2^{-20}	2^{-17}	2^{-26}	2^{-34}	2^{-42}	2^{-50}
	2^{-25}	2^{-22}	2^{-33}	2^{-44}	2^{-55}	2^{-65}

Table 6.1 Overview of δ resulting from Theorem 6.1 for different values of t and ε. For a single secret to be shared with a threshold of $t = 5$ we get an overall robustness of 2^{-65} when 25 bit keys and tags are used.

In summary, the above scheme achieves unconditional security with an information rate of $1/\tilde{O}(\lambda + n)$, with the precise numbers depending on the MAC scheme.

The scheme is robust against a rushing adversary. However, it neither provides homomorphic features nor any verifiability guarantees.

To make the analysis more concrete we show the result based on a practical instantiation. An information-theoretic MAC scheme $\mathsf{Mac} : \mathbb{F} \times \mathbb{F}^2 \to \mathbb{F}$ over a finite field $\mathbb{F}$ in the form of $(m, (\alpha, \beta)) \mapsto \alpha \cdot m + \beta$ is ε-secure with $\varepsilon = 1/2^\ell$. However, if shorter tag has to be produced from larger input messages, batching in the form of polynomial hashing has to be used. The MAC becomes

$$\mathsf{Mac} : \mathbb{F}^d \times \mathbb{F}^2 \to \mathbb{F}, ((m_1, \ldots, m_d), (\alpha, \beta)) \mapsto \sum_{k=1}^{d} \alpha^i \cdot m_i + \beta$$

with $\varepsilon = d/|\mathbb{F}| = d/2^\ell$ as shown in [19].

Now, let ℓ be the size of tag and key of a MAC working in $GF(2^\ell)$ which can be applied to arbitrary input size d fields of $GF(2^d)$ with $2^d > n$, we can derive concrete configurations for an envisaged robustness δ. Setting λ such that $\delta = 2^{-\lambda}$, we get

$$\ell = \lceil \log(t+1) + \log(d) + 2/(t+1)(\lambda + \log(e)) \rceil,$$

which gives the share overhead in bits attached to each d-bit Shamir share as

$$3n\ell \leq 12\lambda + 3n(\log(t+1) + \log(d) + 3).$$

In general, it can be shown that a robust secret sharing scheme with $\delta < 2^{-\lambda}$ and $n = 2t + 1$ requires a minimum share size of $|s| + \lambda$ [14, 36]. While the scheme above only achieves $|s| + \tilde{O}(\lambda + n)$, there is further works that improve over this complexity. Cramer et al. [49] as well as Cheraghchi [44] consider a *ramp* setting where there is a gap between the privacy and the reconstruction threshold: namely, while at least $(\frac{1}{2} + \alpha)n$ shares are required to reconstruct for some $\alpha > 0$, only at most $(\frac{1}{2} - \alpha)n$ servers may be corrupted. Somewhat surprisingly, in this setting the size of the shares can even be *smaller* than the size of the secret to be shared. Lewko and Pasko [14] proposed an almost optimal scheme, where the shares have size $|s| + \tilde{O}(\lambda)$. However, they only consider *local adversaries*; that is, in contrast to the typical and stronger model with a monolithic adversary that controls all corrupted devices, the single servers are here assumed to be corrupted by independent adversaries which may not alter their shares depending on the behavior of the other adversaries. Recent results in RSS have further improved in space efficiency [15, 63]. The most optimal scheme so far was proposed by Manurangsi et al. [102], which has share size of $m + O(\lambda \log n(\log n + \log m))$ bits and also polynomial-time sharing and reconstruction.

6.2 Computationally Secure Approaches

If one is aiming for computational privacy only, it is possible to significantly reduce the overhead of the construction by Cevallos et al. [38]. Namely, instead of using a keyed MAC, one can simply compute a hash of each share, which is then distributed among the parties P_i. This distribution is done such that only $t + 1$ honestly returned parts are necessary to reconstruct the hash value. Doing so, the reconstruction algorithm can then check which shares of the secret were returned honestly, and the secret can be recomputed. This scheme was originally proposed by Krawczyk [92].

Reconstructing the hash value from partially altered parts can be achieved by using an error correcting code, where we denote the coding function by C and the decoding function by D. On a high level, such a code maps strings of length j into a sequence of n strings in a way that allows to reconstruct a message if at least $\frac{d-1}{2}$ indices have not been modified. Here, d is the distance of the code. As we assume up to d malicious shares, we require the code to have $d \geq 2t + 1$.

The algorithms of the scheme are defined in the following. Let therefore (share′, reconstruct′) be a secret sharing scheme according to Definition 4.2, potentially the scheme from Section 4.2.

Algorithm 6.2: Krawczyk [92]

share: On input a secret s, the algorithm performs in two steps:

1. It first shares the secret as $(\sigma'_1, \ldots, \sigma'_n) \xleftarrow{s} \text{share}'(s)$.
2. It then fingerprints each share. That is, for each $i = 1, \ldots, n$, it applies the error correcting code to $\text{Hash}(\sigma'_i)$ by computing

$$(\sigma'_{i,1}, \ldots, \sigma'_{i,n}) \xleftarrow{s} \text{C}(\text{Hash}(\sigma'_i)).$$

The algorithm outputs $\sigma_i := (\sigma'_i, \sigma'_{1,i}, \ldots, \sigma'_{n,i})$ for all $i = 1, \ldots, n$.

reconstruct: Upon receiving inputs of the form $\sigma_i := (\sigma'_i, \sigma'_{1,i}, \ldots, \sigma'_{n,i})$ for $i = 1, \ldots, n$, this algorithm proceeds as follows:

1. For each $i = 1, \ldots, n$, the algorithm uses the error correcting code to reconstruct the fingerprint of σ'_i, i.e., it computes $f_i := \text{D}(\sigma'_{i,1}, \ldots, \sigma'_{i,n})$.
2. For each $i = 1, \ldots, n$, the algorithm next checks whether σ'_i was correctly returned by checking whether $f_i \overset{?}{=} \text{Hash}(\sigma'_i)$. If this is the case, it adds i to the initially empty set $\mathcal{I}$.
3. The algorithm now uses the correctly returned shares to reconstruct the secret by running $s' \xleftarrow{s} \text{reconstruct}'(\{(i, \sigma'_i) : i \in \mathcal{I}\})$, and outputs s'.

The following theorem can now be shown [92]:

Theorem 6.2 *Let t and $n \geq 2t + 1$ be integers, and* (share′, reconstruct′) *be a secure secret sharing scheme. Let further* (C, D) *be an error correcting code with distance*

$d \geq 2t + 1$ *as described above, and* Hash $: \{0, 1\}^* \rightarrow \{0, 1\}^j$ *be a random oracle.* *Then, the above scheme is a robust secret sharing scheme for the same message* *space as* (share′, reconstruct′).

The above scheme offers conditional security guarantees. Regarding its information rate, it is easy to see that it is asymptotically space optimal if the scheme (share′, reconstruct′) is. Namely, the shares of the entire scheme consist of the shares of this subroutine, plus a constant-size overhead. This is, because C is executed only on the hash of the input, and thus independent of the actual size of the secret s. Furthermore, the scheme is robust against rushing adversaries. Finally, the scheme neither provides homomorphic nor verifiability guarantees.

Chapter 7
Verifiable Secret Sharing

So far, we always assumed that the adversary is not able to corrupt the dealer of a secret message. However, this might sometimes be an unrealistic assumption, e.g., in the case of corrupted devices that might modify messages sent to the network. By sending inconsistent shares to the different P_i, it might be possible that the content of the reconstructed file suddenly depends on the servers selected to retrieve the shares from – a behavior that is clearly unwanted for obvious reasons. *Verifiable secret sharing* (or VSS for short), first introduced by Chor et al. [45], therefore also gives security guarantees if the dealer is corrupt. That is, a VSS scheme allows the parties to jointly check the consistency of the shares they received, such that a user is guaranteed that he will receive the same secret from any possible sufficiently large subset of shares.

As VSS schemes are often used as building blocks for higher-level cryptographic primitives such as secure multi-party computation, their definition differs slightly from the definition used so far in this document. Namely, it is assumed that instead of a user downloading sufficiently many shares and trying to reconstruct the secret value, for reconstruction every party broadcasts its share to all other parties in the system. Now, assuming that at most t parties *including the dealer* may be corrupted, it needs to be guaranteed that after this broadcast messages, every honest party will consistently output the same secret.

However, in our use case of a secure distributed storage system it would be unnatural to let all nodes reconstruct the secret every time a user wants to access his files. Actually, in order to guarantee data privacy it is of key importance that this is not the case and only an authorized user should be able to reconstruct the secret during the execution of a read operation. We therefore modify the standard definition found in the literature to fit our specific needs.

Definition 7.1 A *verifiable secret sharing scheme for storage solutions* is an (n, k)-threshold secret sharing scheme, where correctness and privacy only have to hold for honest dealers. Furthermore, share may in general be an interactive protocol between the dealer and the parties now, where each P_i at the end of the protocol decides whether or not to accept the share.

Furthermore, the following additional security property has to be satisfied:

S. Krenn and T. Lorünser, *An Introduction to Secret Sharing*,
SpringerBriefs in Information Security and Cryptography,
https://doi.org/10.1007/978-3-031-28161-7_7

Commitment: The scheme is (n, k, t, l)-committing, if at the end of the sharing
phase, for a maximum of t corrupted parties including the dealer, there exists a
unique $s^* \in S \cup \{\bot\}$ such that every set of at least l shares reconstructs to the
same s^*.

For non-verifiable secret sharing schemes, we only had to distinguish between protocols that are private against computationally bounded or unbounded adversaries.
Now, for VSS, we also have to classify the schemes according to the computational
power of the malicious dealer.

Solutions that are unconditionally private and unconditionally committing have
been proposed in the literature, e.g., Fitzi et al. [66], Gennaro et al. [71], or Katz et
al. [88]. However, if the scheme is intended to be perfectly complete, those two goals
can only be achieved simultaneously as long as less than one third of the parties is
corrupted, i.e., if $t < n/3$ [9, 58]. Moreover, higher efficiency can be achieved if one
is willing to assume a computationally limited adversary.

In the following, we will therefore mainly focus on schemes that are private against
a potentially unbounded attacker, but only committing against a computationally
bounded attacker. That is, while the privacy is guaranteed unconditionally, breaking
the commitment property might be possible if the adversary is able to break a
computational assumption at the time of sharing the secret. We believe that this is a
reasonable compromise, as estimating the long-term development of an adversary's
computational power is dangerous and error-prone, while estimating the current
computational power of an attacker is doable.

7.1 Verifiable Secret Sharing in Synchronous Networks

All schemes presented in the following section assume a synchronous communication
model. That is, the protocols presented in this section are assumed to be executed
in rounds, and a protocol phase only starts after the previous round has successfully
ended. Such protocols in particular make sense in high-speed networks with very
little latency and nodes operating at roughly the same speed. Verifiable secret sharing
schemes designed for asynchronous networks will be discussed in the next section.

7.1.1 High Efficiency if Only Few Servers are Corrupted

Pedersen [111] proposed a *non-interactive* verifiable secret sharing scheme. That
is, during the verification phase of the shares, the different parties do not need to
communicate with each other, which is very suitable, e.g., in the case of limited or
expensive bandwidth between different parties.

On a high level, the scheme is an extension of Shamir's scheme, cf. Section 4.1.
The dealer additionally computes an unconditionally hiding commitment to the
secret in a group where the discrete logarithm assumption holds. It further also

shares the randomness used in this commitment among the parties, and broadcasts additional commitments of the coefficients of the polynomials used to share s and the randomness to all parties. The parties can now check that their share is consistent with these broadcasted commitments by simply evaluating the respective polynomials in the exponent.

In the following description, $\mathcal{G}$ is a cyclic group of prime order q, and g, h are randomly chosen system parameters such that $\langle g \rangle = \langle h \rangle = \mathcal{G}$. To achieve maximum efficiency, the space of secrets is defined to be $\mathbb{Z}_q$; however, the scheme also works for any arbitrary subset at the costs of a decreasing secret/share size ratio.

The algorithms of the scheme are now defined as follows:

Algorithm 7.1: Pedersen [111]

share: On input $s \in \mathcal{S} := \mathbb{Z}_q$, this protocol consists of the following steps:

1. The dealer:
   - first computes a Pedersen commitment (cf. Section 2.3.4) to s, i.e., it chooses $r \xleftarrow{\$} \mathbb{Z}_q$ and sets $c_0 = g^s h^r$;
   - then chooses $a_1, \ldots, a_{k-1}, b_1, \ldots, b_{k-1} \xleftarrow{\$} \mathbb{Z}_q$ with $a_{k-1} \neq 0$, and defines:

     $$f(x) := a_{k-1}x^{k-1} + \cdots + a_1 x + s \quad \text{and} \quad g(x) := b_{k-1}x^{k-1} + \cdots + b_1 x + r .$$

     Furthermore, it computes commitments $c_i = g^{a_i} h^{b_i}$ for all $i = 1, \ldots, k-1$.
   - It broadcasts $c_0, c_1, \ldots, c_{k-1}$ to all parties, and sends

     $$\sigma_i := (\sigma_i', \sigma_i'') = (f(i), g(i))$$

     to each party P_i.
2. Each party P_i accepts $\sigma_i = (\sigma_i', \sigma_i'')$ if and only if the following equation holds:

   $$g^{\sigma_i'} h^{\sigma_i''} \stackrel{?}{=} \prod_{j=0}^{k-1} c_j^{i^j} . \tag{7.1}$$

   Otherwise, P_i outputs $\sigma_i := \bot$.

reconstruct: Upon input sufficiently many shares $\{(i, \sigma_i) : i \in \mathcal{I}\}$ where $\sigma_i = (\sigma_i', \sigma_i'')$, this algorithm uses, e.g., the Berlekamp-Welch algorithm [135], to reconstruct $f(x)$, and outputs $s' = f(0)$.

We briefly want to argue the completeness property of the above scheme. Clearly, it is sufficient to show that honest parties will always accept shares from an honest dealer, as in this case completeness follows directly from the completeness of Algorithm 4.2. Now, (7.1) can be seen as follows:

$$g^{\sigma_i'} h^{\sigma_i''} = g^{f(i)} h^{g(i)} = g^{s+\sum_{j=1}^{k-1} a_j i^j} h^{r+\sum_{j=1}^{k-1} b_j i^j}$$

$$= g^s h^r \prod_{j=1}^{k-1} g^{a_j i^j} h^{b_j i^j} = c_0 \prod_{j=1}^{k-1} \left(g^{a_j} h^{b_j} \right)^{i^j} = \prod_{j=0}^{k-1} c_j^{i^j} .$$

The proof of the following theorem is straightforward and can be found in the original literature [111].

Theorem 7.1 *For every integers t, k, n such that $k \geq t + 1$ and $n \geq 2t + k$, and every prime $q > n$, the above scheme is a perfectly complete, perfectly private, and computationally $(n, k, t, 2t + k)$-committing verifiable secret sharing scheme for storage solutions under the discrete logarithm assumption in $\mathcal{G}$.*

In summary, the above scheme is thus unconditionally secure. Regarding the information rate, note that after the sharing phase, each party can safely delete the c_i's as well as σ_i'', and only needs to permanently store the value of σ_i' like in Shamir's scheme. Therefore, despite the communicational overhead during the sharing phase, the scheme is ideal in terms of the actual storage requirements, and achieves an information rate of 1. The scheme is computationally committing, yet does not provide any robustness guarantees.

Pedersen's scheme can be seen as the "dual" to Feldman's scheme [64]: while the former is unconditionally private but only computationally committing, the latter is unconditionally committing but only computationally hiding. Feldman's scheme can essentially be obtained by replacing the unconditionally hiding Pedersen commitments in the scheme above by some perfectly complete homomorphic encryption scheme that satisfies the required homomorphic properties, e.g., [70]. However, as argued earlier, we believe that for our use-case unconditional privacy is more important than an unconditional committing property.

Finally, we want to note that in order to reduce the computational and communciational overhead of VSS schemes, batching techniques have been proposed which allow one to simultaneously share and verify a set of secret values [6, 94].

7.1.2 Higher Security Comes at a Price

Backes et al. [2] present a protocol for which the reconstruction is guaranteed to be efficient even if n only satisfies $n \geq 2t + 1$. The protocol can be seen as an extension of the protocol described above. The protocol requires an additional round of communication in the sharing phase, and thus it is not non-interactive any more. However, this can be shown to be necessary, as non-interactive verifiable secret sharing schemes are impossible in the considered adversary model for any $n \leq 3t$ [2].

In the following, we concretely instantiate the original protocol with Pedersen commitments [111], cf. also Section 2.3.4.

Algorithm 7.2: Backes et al. [2]

share: On input a secret $s \in \mathbb{Z}_q$, the protocol proceeds in the following steps:

1. The dealer:
   - first computes a Pedersen commitment (cf. Section 2.3.4) to s, i.e., it chooses $r \xleftarrow{\$} \mathbb{Z}_q$ and sets $c_0 = g^s h^r$;
   - then chooses $a_1, \ldots, a_{k-1}, b_1, \ldots, b_{k-1} \xleftarrow{\$} \mathbb{Z}_q$ with $a_{k-1} \neq 0$, and defines:

     $$f(x) := a_{k-1}x^{k-1} + \cdots + a_1 x + s \quad \text{and} \quad g(x) := b_{k-1}x^{k-1} + \cdots + b_1 x + r.$$

     Furthermore, it computes commitments $c_i = g^{a_i} h^{b_i}$ for all $i = 1, \ldots, k-1$.
   - It broadcasts $c_0, c_1, \ldots, c_{k-1}$ to all parties, and sends $(f_i, r_i) := (f(i), g(i))$ to each party P_i.
2. Each party P_i chooses $(p_i, q_i), (v_i, w_i) \xleftarrow{\$} \mathbb{Z}_q^2$ and broadcasts $c_{p,i} := g^{p_i} h^{q_i}$ and $c_{v,i} := g^{v_i} h^{w_i}$. It further sends (p_i, q_i) and (v_i, w_i) to the dealer.
3. For each $i = 1, \ldots, n$, the dealer checks whether $c_{p,i}$ and $c_{v,i}$ are consistent with the received (p_i, q_i) and (v_i, w_i), respectively. If they are, the dealer broadcasts $\alpha_i := f_i + p_i$ and $\beta_i := r_i + v_i$; otherwise, the dealer broadcasts (f_i, r_i).
4. Each party P_i checks whether:

   $$g^{f_i} h^{r_i} \stackrel{?}{=} \prod_{j=0}^{k-1} c_j^{i^j}.$$

   If it is, it is **happy** and does nothing; otherwise, it is **unhappy** and broadcasts (p_i, q_i) and (v_i, w_i).
5. Now, every party P_l locally performs the following local computations:
   - It outputs $\sigma_l := \bot$ and halts, if:
     - the dealer broadcasted (f_i, r_i) for some i such that $g^{f_i} h^{r_i} \neq \prod_{j=0}^{k-1} c_j^{i^j}$; or if
     - the dealer broadcasted (α_i, β_i), and P_i broadcasted (p_i, q_i) and (v_i, w_i) such that $c_{p,i} = g^{p_i} h^{q_i}$ and $c_{v,i} = g^{v_i} h^{w_i}$, but $g^{\alpha_i - p_i} h^{\beta_i - v_i} \neq \prod_{j=0}^{k-1} c_i^{i^j}$.
   - It discards an **unhappy** P_i, if it broadcasted (p_i, q_i) and (v_i, w_i) such that $c_{p,i} \neq g^{p_i} h^{q_i}$ or $c_{v,i} \neq g^{v_i} h^{w_i}$. Let Q_l denote the set of non-discarded parties.
   - Depending on its state, it now computes its share as:
     - If $P_l \in Q$ is **happy**, it outputs $\sigma_l := (f_l, r_l, (c_m)_{m=0}^{k-1}, Q_l)$ as received from the dealer in (1).
     - If $P_l \in Q$ is **unhappy**, it outputs $\sigma_l := (f_l, r_l, (c_m)_{m=0}^{k-1}, Q_l)$ if it was broadcasted by the dealer in (3).
     - Else, P_l outputs $\sigma_l := (\alpha_l - p_l, \beta_l - v_l, (c_m)_{m=0}^{k-1}, Q_l)$

reconstruct: Given as inputs $\{(i, \sigma_i) : i \in \mathcal{I} \wedge \sigma_i \neq \perp\}$ for $|\mathcal{I}| \geq 2k - 1 = 2t + 1$, the algorithm proceeds as follows:

1. It determines the correct set Q and the correct $(c_m)_{m=0}^{k-1}$ by a simple majority vote over the inputs.
2. For each $i \in \mathcal{I}$, it checks whether or not $g^{f_i} h^{r_i} \stackrel{?}{=} \prod_{j=0}^{k-1} c_i^{i^j}$. If yes, (f_i, r_i) is *confirmed*.
3. Given any set of at least k confirmed (f_i, r_i), the algorithm computes the unique interpolation polynomial $f(x)$ of degree $k - 1$ for the (i, f_i).
4. The algorithm finally outputs $s' = f(0)$.

For the proof of the following theorem we refer to the original literature [2].

Theorem 7.2 *For every integers t, k, n such that $k \geq t + 1$ and $n \geq t + k$, the above protocol is a perfectly complete, perfectly private, and computationally $(n, k, t, t+k)$-committing verifiable secret sharing scheme for storage solutions under the discrete logarithm assumption in $\mathcal{G}$.*

In summary, the scheme offers unconditional security and is computationally committing. It has been designed in a synchronous network model, and has been proved secure against non-adaptive adversaries. Furthermore, it is does not provide any robustness guarantees.

Furthermore, the authors provide a protocol which is not based on homomorphic commitments, but we here refrain from presenting this more general protocol because of the additional computational overhead.

7.1.3 Publicly Verifiable Secret Sharing

So far, we always considered VSS schemes where the respective share holders are able to verify the consistency of the distributed shares. Yet, sometimes it may be more practical if this verification could be outsourced to a third party. For instance, in a distributed storage setting, this might be the case if the storage nodes are computationally bounded, or if computation power on the server side is expensive. In this case, it might make sense to use *publicly verifiable secret sharing*, where the dealer reveals enough information to the public such that everybody can verify the consistency of the shares.

In such a scheme, there exists an additional algorithm verify, which takes this published information as input, and which outputs whether or not the shares are indeed consistent.

In the following we will describe a simple and elegant scheme by Schoenmakers [119]. We chose to present this scheme because of its practical importance in the DepSky cloud-of-cloud distributed storage solution [11, 47].

In the description, let G be a cyclic group of prime order q with generator g such that the discrete logarithm assumption holds in G. Let furthermore each party P_i register a public key $v_i := g^{x_i}$ at the dealer, where $x_i \xleftarrow{\$} \mathbb{Z}_q$ is kept secret by P_i. The scheme is then defined as follows:

Algorithm 7.3: Schoenmakers [119]

share: To share a secret $s := g^S$ for some $S \in \mathbb{Z}_q$, the protocol proceeds in the following steps:

1. The dealer:
   - first chooses $a_1, \ldots, a_{k-1} \xleftarrow{\$} \mathbb{Z}_q$ with $a_{k-1} \neq 0$ and defines:

   $$f(x) := a_{k-1}x^{k-1} + \cdots + a_1 x + S.$$

   - Furthermore, it computes $c_0 := g^S$, $c_j := g^{a_j}$ for $j = 1, \ldots, k-1$, and $y_i := v_i^{f(i)}$ for $i = 1, \ldots, n$, and $w_i := \prod_{j=0}^{k-1} c_j^{i^j}$ for all $i = 1, \ldots, n$.
   - It then shows that the encrypted shares are consistent by computing:

   $$\pi \xleftarrow{\$} \mathsf{ZKP}\left[(\phi_1, \ldots, \phi_n) : \bigwedge_{i=1}^{n} \left(w_i = g^{\phi_i} \wedge y_i = v_i^{\phi_i} \right) \right],$$

   using $\phi_i = f(i)$ as witnesses.
   Finally, the dealer makes all $(c_j)_{j=1}^{k-1}$, $(y_i)_{i=1}^{n}$, as well as π public.

2. Each party P_i computes $z_i := y_i^{x_i^{-1}}$, and:

   $$\pi_i \xleftarrow{\$} \mathsf{ZKP}\left[(\chi_i) : v_i = g^{\chi_i} \wedge y_i = z_i^{\chi_i} \right],$$

   using $\chi_i = x_i$ as witness. The party outputs $\sigma_i := (z_i, \pi_i)$.

reconstruct: Having sufficiently many shares $\{(i, \sigma_i) : i \in \mathcal{I}\}$ as input, this algorithm verifies the provided π_i and outputs:

$$s' := \prod_{i \in \mathcal{I}} z_i^{\lambda_i} \quad \text{where} \quad \lambda_i := \prod_{\substack{j \in \mathcal{I} \\ j \neq i}} \frac{j}{j - i}.$$

verify: Everybody can verify the consistency of the dealer's output by recomputing the w_i from the given c_j, and then verifying the validity of π as in Figure 2.2.

We want to note that P_i does not need to store π_i as part of σ_i, but that this proof can be computed on the fly when the share is retrieved. The reason for this presentation was only to keep the reconstruction algorithm as simple as possible.

It is possible to show the following theorem:

Theorem 7.3 *For every integers* t, k, n *such that* $k \geq t + 1$ *and* $n \geq t + k$, *the above protocol is a perfectly complete, computationally private, and computationally* $(n, k, t + k)$-*committing publicly verifiable secret sharing scheme for storage solutions under the discrete logarithm assumption in* $\mathcal{G}$.

In fact one can show that the protocol satisfies a strong commitment property. Namely, it can be shown that not only all sufficiently large sets of shares will recover the same secret s^*, but also that this secret coincides with the secret s the dealer started with.

At first glance, the fact that Algorithm 7.3 distributes a group element with known discrete logarithm instead of $s \in \mathbb{Z}_q$ might let the scheme appear impracticable for storage solutions. To still use it in our setting, one could use the scheme in a similar way as the computationally private construction from Algorithm 4.3. For instance, one could mask the key K of a symmetric cipher similar to the ElGamal encryption scheme [70], by computing Kg^S. Now, the mask g^S could be distributed using Algorithm 7.3, while Kg^S (which does not contain any information about K if g^S is unknown) could be distributed along with the message encrypted under K, using an information dispersal scheme.

Publicly verifiable secret sharing schemes for directly sharing a secret s (and not g^s) were, e.g., given by Fujisaki and Okamoto [69] or Jhanwar et al. [85].

7.2 Verifiable Secret Sharing in Asynchronous Networks

In all protocols so far we assumed a synchronous network model. In particular we assumed that all network messages will be delivered within a bounded time delay. However, in the case of an unstable network, or if the adversary is in (partial) control of the network, this might not always be realistic. We therefore now consider an asynchronous network model, where unbounded delays of network messages can happen. However, we assume that all channels between honest parties are private and authenticated. That is, an adversary may delay or re-order messages sent by honest parties, but it may not read or modify them. Also, the adversary eventually has to deliver all the messages sent by honest parties.

In such a setting, the secret sharing scheme has to satisfy the following properties:

Definition 7.2 An *asynchronous verifiable secret sharing (AVSS) scheme for storage solutions* is a secret sharing scheme according to Definition 7.1 which additionally satisfies the following two properties:

Liveness: If the dealer is honest in the sharing phase, then all honest parties complete the sharing phase.

Agreement: If at least one honest party completes the sharing phase, then all honest parties will eventually complete the sharing phase. Furthermore, if at least l parties subsequently start the reconstruction phase, then the reconstructing party will complete the reconstruction phase.

In the following we detail the scheme proposed by Backes et al. [2], which can be seen as an enhancement of the AVSS scheme by Cachin et al. [31]. The protocol can be shown to satisfy Definition 7.2 if the secret is shared between at least $3t + 1$ parties, which is also known to be the minimum number of required parties to realize AVSS.

As for Algorithm 7.2, the scheme is perfectly private but only computationally committing. The communication complexity of the scheme can easily be seen to be $O(n^3)$, which is significantly better than for all schemes achieving a perfect commitment property [34, 35, 108, 109].

In the following description, let (KGen, Commit, Verify) be a commitment scheme, and let $K \xleftarrow{\$} \mathsf{KGen}(1^\lambda)$ be common input to all parties.

Algorithm 7.4: Backes et al. [2]

---

share: On input a secret $s \in \mathbb{Z}_q$, the protocol proceeds in the following steps:

1. The dealer:
   - First chooses a random symmetric bivariate polynomial $f(x, y) \xleftarrow{\$} \mathbb{Z}_q[x, y]$ of degree t such that $f(0, 0) = s$.
   - Next, it defines $f_{i,j} := f(i, j)$ and computes $(c_{i,j}, d_{i,j}) \xleftarrow{\$} \mathsf{Commit}(f_{i,j})$ for all $1 \le j \le i \le n$. Furthermore, it assigns $(c_{j,i}, d_{j,i}) := (c_{i,j}, d_{i,j})$ for $1 \le i < j \le n$. Let C be the $n \times n$ matrix formed by the $c_{i,j}$.
   - It sends $(\mathsf{Send}, C, f_i(x), d_i(x))$ to P_i, where $f_i(x) := f(x, i)$, and $d_i(x)$ is the polynomial of degree $n - 1$ defined by $d_i(j) = d_{i,j}$ for all $1 \le j \le n$.
2. Each party P_i does the following:
   - Upon receiving a message of the form $(\mathsf{Send}, C, f_i(x), d_i(x))$ from the dealer, it sends (echo, C) to all P_j if C is a symmetric $n \times n$ matrix and if $\mathsf{Verify}(f_i(j), c_{i,j}, d_{i,j}) \overset{?}{=} 1$.
   - Upon receiving (echo, C) from at least $2t+1$ parties (potentially including itself) satisfying that C was the same as the one received from the dealer, send $(\mathsf{ready}, \mathsf{share\text{-}holder}, C)$ to every P_j, if P_i has already sent out echo messages.
   - If you have not sent out an ready messages before, do the following:
     a. Upon receiving ready messages from at least $t+1$ parties satisfying that the received C was the same as the one received from the dealer, send $(\mathsf{ready}, \mathsf{share\text{-}holder}, C)$ to every P_j, if P_i has already sent out echo messages.
     b. Upon receiving ready messages from at least $t + 1$ parties satisfying that the received C are all equal but do not match the value received from the dealer, update the local copy of C with this new matrix, delete everything else received from the dealer, and send $(\mathsf{ready}, \star, C)$ to every P_j.

- Upon receiving **ready** messages from at least $2t + 1$ parties satisfying that the received C was the same as the local copy, and at least $t + 1$ of these messages contained **share-holder**, agree on C.
- Finally, output $\sigma_i := (f_i(x), d_i(x), C)$ if (**ready**, **share-holder**, C) has been sent before; otherwise, output $\sigma_i := \bot$.

reconstruct: Upon requesting shares from at least $3t + 1$ parties, this algorithm proceeds as follows:

1. It waits for at least $t + 1$ shares σ_i with the same C, where each $f_i(x)$ is a polynomial of degree t, each $d_i(x)$ is a polynomial of degree $n - 1$, and $\mathsf{Verify}(f_i(k), c_{i,k}, d_i(k)) \overset{?}{=} 1$ for all $k = 1, \ldots, n$.
2. It then uses these $f_i(x)$ to reconstruct the bivariate polynomial $f(x, y)$.
3. The algorithm finally outputs $s' = f(0, 0)$.

For the proof of the following theorem we refer to the original literature [2].

Theorem 7.4 *For every integers t, n such that $n \geq 3t + 1$, the above protocol is a perfectly complete, perfectly private, and computationally $(n, t + 1, t, 3t + 1)$-committing asynchronous verifiable secret sharing scheme for storage solutions if the deployed commitment scheme is perfectly hiding and computationally binding.*

A large additional body of work on VSS schemes proven secure in an asynchronous network model have been proposed in the literature, e.g., [8, 46, 110]. We also refer to Chandramouli et al.'s survey on perfectly secure verifiable secret sharing [39].

Chapter 8
Proactive Secret Sharing

Secret sharing as described in Chapter 4 allows to provide confidentiality for data stored. However, an attacker may be *mobile*, as discovered in [107], and break into enough server over time to reconstruct the secret. In some scenarios it might be sufficient to provide confidentiality for a limited time interval only, but not when dealing with highly sensitive data, for instance, military and government secret files, industrial secrets, lawsuits, election data, and medical records. This information requires long-term or even everlasting confidentiality. Therefore, for long-term storage, so called proactive secret sharing schemes were developed where each document is split into shares that are renewed from time to time. Also, in the case of a distributed storage system, the storage providers might change over time, because certain providers discontinue their service, or simply because a new competitor offers the same service at a lower price. In this case simply copying date from one server to the other is not an option, as this would provide the adversary with a much easier target for this particular share.

8.1 Proactive Secret Sharing in Synchronous Networks

Proactive security has been first suggested by Ostrovsky and Yung in [107] in form of a proactive polynomial secret sharing scheme. In [82] Herzberg et al. specialized this notion and introduced the first proactive secret sharing scheme to provide long-term confidentiality in data storage systems. This scheme uses an information theoretically secure and verifiable secret sharing scheme, such as Shamir's Secret Sharing (see Chapter 4), combined with Pedersen's (see Section 2.3.4) or Feldman's [64] commitments. In [127] Stinson and Wei propose a scheme that is unconditionally secure, i.e., the security of the scheme does not rely on any cryptographic assumption. However, the disadvantage of both proposals is that the structure of the shareholders must be maintained. This means that the set of shareholders before and after the share renewal process must be the same. Desmedt and Jajodia [54] improved this approach by showing how to redistribute a secret without recovering

© The Author(s), under exclusive license to Springer Nature Switzerland AG 2023
S. Krenn and T. Lorünser, *An Introduction to Secret Sharing*,
SpringerBriefs in Information Security and Cryptography,
https://doi.org/10.1007/978-3-031-28161-7_8

it such that changes on the access structure are possible. This allows to add or re-move shareholders, e.g. reboot or reinstall compromised servers, and to change the number of shares needed to reconstruct the secret. Then, Wong et al. [136] further developed this scheme by combining it with verifiable secret sharing. It follows that assuming the majority of the old shareholders to be trustworthy, the new share-holders can verify the validity of the shares received. This not only protects against mobile adversaries, but also against active (or Byzantine [96]) adversaries that are able to alter or replace messages. Nevertheless, correctness of the new shares is only guaranteed if all new shareholders are trustworthy and verify the data received. Therefore, Gupta and Gopinath [78] further improved this protocol by a complaint mechanism requiring only a majority of the new shareholders to be reliable. However, both verifiable schemes use Feldman's commitments that are only computationally hiding to generate the public audit information. In their revised protocol from 2007 [79] they use Pedersen commitments, therefore achieving information-theoretic se-curity. Another interesting work is the proactive secret sharing scheme presented by Sun et al. in [128]. Their scheme is based on elliptic curve cryptography and is therefore more efficient. However, it reveals information about the data shared to a computationally unbounded attacker, which is why an efficient solution that provides information-theoretic security is still an interesting topic for future work.

In the following we will briefly describe the solution presented by Gupta and Gopinath. In the description, we will concentrate on showing how the data is dis-tributed, how the shares are renewed, and how the document can be reconstructed. For details regarding the complaint mechanism and the security analysis, we refer to [79]. We assume that $(q, \mathcal{G}, g, h) \xleftarrow{s} \mathsf{KGen}(1^\lambda)$ is a common input to all parties, where KGen is the key generation algorithm of the Pedersen commitment scheme, cf. Section 2.3.4.

Algorithm 8.1: Gupta and Gopinath [79]

---

share: On input a secret $s \in \mathbb{Z}_q$, this protocol works identically like the one in Algorithm 7.1, except that each party in additional stores c_0 as part of σ_i. Furthermore, in the case that $\sigma_i = \bot$, a complaint mechanism described in [79] is used.

renew: To renew and redistribute the shares to a new set of n' shareholders such that $k' \leq n'$ shares are needed to reconstruct secret s, the old shareholders jointly compute two new polynomials f' and g' such that $f'(0) = s$ and $g'(0) = r$. More precisely, the following steps are performed.

1. Each old shareholder i, for $i = 1, \ldots, n$, applies the secret sharing procedure to its shares s_i, r_i. In particular, it generates two polynomials

$$f_i'(x) = s_i + a_{i,1}'x + \ldots + a_{i,k'-1}'x^{k'-1} \quad \text{and}$$
$$g_i'(x) = r_i + b_{i,1}'x + \ldots + b_{i,k'-1}'x^{k'-1}$$

of degree $k' - 1$, where the coefficients $a'_{i,1}, \ldots, a'_{i,k'-1}, b'_{i,1}, \ldots, b'_{i,k'-1} \in \mathbb{Z}_q$ are chosen uniformly at random.

It then sends to each new shareholder j, for $j = 1, \ldots, n'$, a pair of sub-shares $(s^*_{i,j}, r^*_{i,j})$, where $s^*_{i,j} = f'_i(j)$ and $r^*_{i,j} = g'_i(j)$.

2. To generate the witness, each old shareholder i computes a commitment

$$v'_{i,l} = g^{a'_{i,l}} h^{b'_{i,l}} \quad \text{for} \quad l = 1, \ldots, k' - 1,$$

to each pair of coefficients and broadcasts this data together with witness c_0, and the commitment to its own shares $c'_{i,0} = g^{s_i} h^{r_i}$.

3. Each new shareholder j verifies the correctness of all received shares by checking whether for all $i = 1, \ldots, n$ the following equation holds.

$$g^{s^*_{i,j}} h^{r^*_{i,j}} \stackrel{?}{=} c'_{i,0} \prod_{l=1}^{k-1} v'_{i,l}{}^{j^l} \tag{8.1}$$

Furthermore, it can check whether the set of old shares $\{s_1, s_2, \ldots, s_n\}$ was correct using the broadcast commitments $c'_{i,0} = g^{s_i} h^{r_i}$. To do so the shareholder verifies for each k-subset $\mathcal{B}_u$, where $u = 1, 2, \ldots, K$ (for further details how K is chosen see [79]) of old shareholders that

$$c_0 = g^s h^r \equiv \prod_{i \in \mathcal{B}_u} c'_{i,0}{}^{b_i} \equiv \prod_{i \in \mathcal{B}_u} (g^{s_i} h^{r_i})^{b_i} \equiv g^{\sum_{i \in \mathcal{B}_u} s_i b_i} h^{\sum_{i \in \mathcal{B}_u} r_i b_i}, \tag{8.2}$$

where $b_i = \prod_{l \in \mathcal{B}_u, l \neq i} \frac{l}{l-i}$. Note that $\sum_{i \in \mathcal{B}_u} s_i b_i$ is the Lagrange interpolation formula where s_i are shares to s from subset $\mathcal{B}_u$. If the shareholder found wrongly generated shares this can be resolved using the complaint mechanism.

4. Each new shareholder j takes a subset $\mathcal{B}^*$ for which (8.1) and (8.2) hold and generates its pair of shares (s'_j, r'_j) by computing

$$s'_j = \sum_{i \in \mathcal{B}^*} s^*_{i,j} b_i \quad \text{and} \quad r'_j = \sum_{i \in \mathcal{B}^*} r^*_{i,j} b_i,$$

where $b_i = \prod_{l \in \mathcal{B}_u, l \neq i} \frac{l}{l-i}$.

It then stores its share pair together with witness c_0.

reconstruct: To reconstruct a secret s the dealer performs a Lagrange interpolation on k shares. More precisely, the following steps are performed.

1. The dealer requests the share pair (s_i, r_i) from each shareholder i, for $i = 1, \ldots, n$ together with witness $c_0 = g^s h^r$.

2. The dealer generates a commitment $c'_{i,0} = g^{s_i} h^{r_i}$ to each share pair and checks for each k-subset of shareholders $\mathcal{B}_u$, $u = 0, \ldots, k - 1$, whether (8.2), $c_0 \stackrel{?}{=} \prod_{i \in \mathcal{B}_u} c'_{i,0}{}^{b_i}$ with $b_i = \prod_{l \in \mathcal{B}_u, l \neq i} \frac{l}{l-i}$, holds.

3. The dealer takes the first set $\mathcal{B}^*$ for which this test succeeds and reconstructs s using the Lagrange interpolation, i.e., computes $\sum_{i \in \mathcal{B}_u} s_i b_i$, where $b_i = \prod_{l \in \mathcal{B}_u, l \neq i} \frac{l}{l-i}$.

Theorem 8.1 *For every integers t, n such that $n \geq 2t + 1$, the above protocol ensures correctness of the shares generated and provides everlasting confidentiality for the data stored.*

8.2 Proactive Secret Sharing in Asynchronous Networks

Another very important requirement for the schemes presented in the last section is that the system is synchronized, i.e., all parties can access a common clock and send their messages simultaneously in one round of the scheme. Note that, in practice networks are usually asynchronous. This means that there is no common global clock and there exist no upper bounds on message delivery delays and processor execution speeds. Thus, the time interval after which a share renewal has to be performed needs to be defined in terms of events in the schemes themselves. There are three solutions that address this aspect: the protocol proposed by Cachin et al. [31], the so called Asynchronous Proactive Secret Sharing (APSS) scheme introduced by Zhou et al. [140], and the Mobile Proactive Secret Sharing (MPSS) scheme developed by Schultz and Liskov [120, 121]. All these solutions use a different proactive secret sharing scheme. In the following, we will provide some high-level information about their construction. Afterwards, we concentrate on their definition of timing and how the communication is organized, since this are the critical aspects in asynchronous networks. Note that the methods proposed to address the asynchronism can be applied to other proactive secret sharing schemes as well.

Cachin et al. [31] developed the first proactive secret sharing scheme designed for the asynchronous model. Their approach is based on resharing the shares of a secret and combining the resulting sub-shares to form new shares. Although this might allow for changes on the access structure, this issue is not addressed in their work. Instead, in APSS such changes are supported. However, their construction is based on an exclusive-or sharing scheme rather than on Shamir's secret sharing. This approach is simpler, but results in exponentially large shares which is why the communication complexity to refresh those shares is exponential in the number of shareholders. Performance measurements showed that this is only suitable for small thresholds [43]. The latest work in the field of proactive secret sharing is MPSS. It builds on the scheme proposed by Herzberg et al., but with an extra twist that allows for changes on the access structure. Their current approach uses Feldman's commitments that only provide computational confidentiality. However, the alternative use of Pedersen commitments is possible.

Besides using a different proactive secret sharing scheme, these solutions also have different methods to define the time interval between two share renewal processes.

In the protocol proposed by Cachin et al. time intervals are defined by a single time signal called *clock tick*. Upon initialization of the protocol, the server sends a *clock tick* to itself. Then, whenever such *clock tick* is received the server re-sends this message over the network to itself to receive it as its next *clock tick*. This allows for defining the local phase of an uncorrupted server as the number of clock ticks received so far. However, the authors assume that honest servers communicate in the same *local phase* and that these messages are delivered in the same local phase as they are sent. The drawback of this approach is that messages still might be delivered with arbitrary delay. Therefore, the share renewal process might take longer than expected and shares might have a longer lifetime than what is recommended to ensure confidentiality in the presence of a mobile adversary. Furthermore, this scheme relies on several sub-protocols, including a robust threshold signature scheme and a threshold coin toss protocol, which may be challenging to implement efficiently.

In APPS the authors refer to the lifetime of a share as *window of vulnerability*. This starts at the beginning of the share renewal process, where the share is generated, and ends at the end of the next share renewal process, where the share is deleted. Assume the share should not exist for a time frame longer than $\mathcal{W}$. Then, in synchronous systems, the periods of time after which a share renewal is triggered $\mathcal{I}$ is set to $\mathcal{I} = \mathcal{W} - \delta$ with $\delta \ll \mathcal{W}$. Thus, shortly before a mobile attacker might be able to collect enough shares the shares are renewed. In asynchronous networks $\mathcal{I}$ should be set to $\mathcal{W} - \Delta$, where Δ is a conservative estimate on the duration of the share renewal procedure. This ensures that the shares are renewed in time. In addition, the clock differences among the correct servers must be taken into account. A clock synchronization protocol can be used to keep the local clocks on correct servers loosely synchronized. Assume that σ is a conservative bound on clock differences. Then, according to its local clock, the share renewal should be invoked on a server after the time interval $\mathcal{W} - \Delta - \sigma$ after the last share renewal. This approach addresses the requirement that shares must be renewed and old shares must be deleted before a mobile adversary is able to collect enough shares to reconstruct the secret.

In MPSS the time interval is defined as local epochs, such that an honest server is in local epoch e if it has secret shares associated with epoch e. It leaves epoch e after the share renewal when it wipes these shares from its memory and is no longer able to recover it. In addition, the system is in epoch e from the moment the first honest node enters the epoch until the last honest node leaves the epoch. Each group member in epoch e can independently initiate the share renewal protocol after the intended epoch duration has passed, according to its local clock. There are two main differences between this solution and APPS. First, the communication only consists of point-to-point messages. This allows an adversary to attack this system by deciding when a message is delivered, and especially which message is delivered. On the other hand MPSS does not require the existence of a broadcast channel. Another is that they provide a way to handle accusations, i.e., one party claims that another party is malicious. This allows to deal with up to t malicious sender and t malicious receiver parties. Note that also the symmetric proactive secret sharing protocol by Gupta and Gopinath requires only a majority amongst the recipients to be honest and allows to change the access structure. Thus, an interesting future work would be to analyze which of these two solutions provide a better performance. An indicator that Gupta and Gopinath provide the more efficient approach is that the share renewal procedure of MPSS consists of two rounds. In the first round the parties agree on the polynomials used for resharing and in the second round the actual share renewal is performed. Furthermore, to decrease the threshold MPSS requires the parties to store and correspondingly to renew additional shares for each secret. On the other hand, the scheme by Gupta and Gopinath requires a synchronous network and it is not clear to what extend their approach can be transferred to systems that do not provide a common clock.

In addition to model the time, the share renewal process has to be extended by a handshake protocol. This ensures, for instance, that old shares are not deleted before a sufficiently large set of new shares is available. As an example, in the following we present the handshake protocol used by ASSP.

Assume a dealer distributes a secret to n parties P_i for $i = 1, \ldots, n$ such that it can only be reconstructed if t of these parties collaborate. Then, the share renewal protocol is started by a coordinator who broadcasts an `init` message containing a label to the shared secret. To ensure consistency, i.e., the servers use the same set of subshares to construct the new shares, each share is accompanied with a version number. Furthermore, for ease of simplicity the authors allow all servers to act as coordinators. To renew the shares the following steps are performed.

- After receiving an `init` message the parties start to generate and distribute new sub-shares.
- Upon receiving new sub-shares, each party checks them for validity and responds with a `verified` message to the sender.
- Once a party received at least $2t - 1$ correctly signed `verified` messages it considers its share as certified and sends a `certified` message to the coordinator.
- After the coordinator collected $l = \binom{n}{t-1}$ `certified` messages it sends a `select` message to the parties.
- Upon receiving a `select` message, each party checks if it has received all sub-shares needed to compute the new share. If this is not the case, it sends a `recovery` message to all other parties and requests the missing sub-shares. If the party has enough sub-shares to compute its new share then it sends a `completed` message to the coordinator.
- After the coordinator received at least $2t - 1$ `completed` messages it broadcast the message `done`.
- Upon receiving a valid `done` message, i.e., containing at least $2t - 1$ `complete` messages, a party deletes its old share.

Chapter 9
Advanced Topics

This introduction to secret sharing is aiming at giving a systematic overview over existing variants of secret sharing. While mainly focusing on well-established types of protocols, the following section gives an overview over further topics, which are still in relatively early stages and under active research and development. The purpose of this chapter is therefore to provide a broad overview and point the interested reader to the relevant original literature, rather than describing all aspects in full detail.

9.1 Function and Homomorphic Secret Sharing

Function secret sharing (FSS), introduced by Boyle et al. [21, 22, 24, 26, 27], is a natural generalization of additive (or more generally, linear) secret sharing schemes, in the sense that it does not only allow for securely sharing individual values s, but entire functions. That is, for a function $f : \mathcal{D} \rightarrow \mathcal{G}$ mapping elements of some domain $\mathcal{D}$ to elements of some abelian group $\mathcal{G}$, a function secret sharing scheme enables one to derive functions $f_1, \ldots, f_n$ described by succinct keys $k_0, \ldots, k_n$ such that $f_1(x) + \cdots + f_n(x) = f(x)$ for all possible inputs $x \in \mathcal{D}$. Furthermore, it must be guaranteed that without access to sufficiently many k_i, the shared function remains hidden, where typically it is assumed that this needs to be the case as long as at least one k_j is secure.

In contrast to most other secret sharing schemes presented in the previous sections, it is not possible to perfectly hide f when aiming for succinct keys k_i, as in this case each function share would need to consist of $|\mathcal{D}|$ elements of $\mathcal{G}$ [24]. However, when also taking computationally hiding FSS schemes into consideration, significantly more compact solutions exist for interesting classes $\mathcal{F}$ of functions. An often considered class of functions is that of distributed point functions [74], which give raise to multi-server private information retrieval (PIRs) protocols or private keyword search. These are functions of the form $f_{\alpha,\beta}$ satisfying:

© The Author(s), under exclusive license to Springer Nature Switzerland AG 2023
S. Krenn and T. Lorünser, *An Introduction to Secret Sharing*,
SpringerBriefs in Information Security and Cryptography,
https://doi.org/10.1007/978-3-031-28161-7_9

$$f_{\alpha,\beta}(x) = \begin{cases} \beta & \text{if } x = \alpha, \\ 0 & \text{else.} \end{cases}$$

For the case of $n = 2$, such and certain other basic functions can efficient be instantiated from any pseudorandom generator or a one-way function [24, 74]. When using assumptions such as learning with errors (LWE) which are known to also imply fully homomorphic encryption (FHE) [72], efficient FSS schemes for any polynomial time function can be constructed [24, 57]. Finally, certain types of functions are also known to be achievable from other assumptions such as the Decisional Diffie-Hellman assumption [25]. Several extensions to FSS exist, including, e.g., verifiable FSS for certain types of functions such as distributed point functions [37].

A notion closely related and in a certain way dual to FSS is that of homomorphic secret sharing (HSS) [25, 28]. Homomorphic secret sharing allows for locally evaluating a function on (one or more) shared inputs, resulting in short shares of the result. That is, for a secret s with shares $\sigma_1, \ldots, \sigma_n$ and a function f, each node can locally perform a computation $\mathsf{Eval}(f, \sigma_i)$, such that upon reconstruction of the resulting shares the dealer obtains $f(s)$ without requiring any further interaction. The duality to FSS can now be seen by reversing the roles of the function f and the secret s. As also discussed by Boyle et al. [28], HSS can offer a viable alternative to FHE, depending on the specific application scenario and its requirements, as it allows to outsource potentially expensive computation queries on distributed data, e.g., in situations where the receiver only holds a constraint device with very limited computation capacity.

Similar to FSS, HSS is currently a very active field of research, and a large body of work on schemes for different classes of functions and under different assumptions has been carried out, e.g., [23, 26, 29, 56, 62], and we refer the interested reader to the original literature for an up-to-date overview of the state of the art.

9.2 Rational and Social Secret Sharing

Rational secret sharing considers the scenario where not a single party fetches all shares to reconstruct the secret, but where all parties holding shares mutually exchange their shares so that every node receives the shared data. Rational secret secret now takes a fundamentally different approach regarding the adversarial model. Namely, instead of distinguishing between honest and malicious nodes in a protocol run, a rational model is applied, which assumes some rational behavior of nodes in the sense that they prefer to receive above all. More precisely, it is assumed that all parties holding shares of a valid sharing are interested in learning the correct result during reconstruction, while no other parties should be able to do so. This leads to a game theoretic view of the reconstruction procedure with interesting results.

Halpern and Teague [80] show that for threshold secret sharing there is no incentive for parties to reveal their share to others in the given model, but instead their best strategy is to not send the share, leading to an impossibility for reconstruction. To see this, consider an (n, k) threshold secret sharing scheme where the shares have been distributed to parties $P_1, \ldots, P_n$. Intuitively, if a party P_i receives at least $k - 1$ shares from other parties, she can reconstruct the secret no matter if she broadcast her own share or not. Furthermore, there are situations where only she learns the secret, i.e., if only $k - 1$ parties broadcast their shares. As a consequence, the preferred strategy of the parties is to not broadcast their own shares, making reconstruction impossible.

In fact, Halpern and Teague proved that in their model no practical protocol exists to assure reconstruction within a bounded running time. However, they present a randomized practical solution with constant expected running time for $n = 3$ and $k \leq 3$, and an extensions to $n > 3$ parties with $3 \leq k \leq n$. Furthermore, the results were also extended to multiparty computation based on secret sharing.

Furthermore, the limitations of $k \geq 3$ were overcome by Gordon and Katz [77]. They showed an efficient and simple protocol for rational secret sharing with two nodes ($n = 2$) which also generalizes to the case of $n \geq 3$ and arbitrary $k \leq n$. Additionally, it introduces a method to overcome the limitation of a continuous involvement of the dealer.

In a nutshell, the protocol works as follows. Similar to Halpern and Teague, the protocol is based on rounds and for simplicity we do not consider active nodes but assume all n nodes are assumed to participate in the reconstruction. In each round the dealer only generates a (n, k) threshold secret sharing of the secret s with probability β, while with probability $1 - \beta$ an invalid sharing is generated. To perfectly hide the type of secret shared in each round, the dealer embeds $s \in S$ into a larger finite field. This can easily be achieved with Shamir secret sharing, by taking a larger field $\mathbb{F}$ containing the subfield $S = \mathbb{F}'$ for sharing s together with invalid secrets $\hat{s} \in \mathbb{F} \setminus S$. Each party begins with a flag all_honest = true. After the secret is freshly shared and distributed to the parties each party broadcasts the share if all_honest = true and waits for incoming shares. If at least $k - 1$ shares where received and a valid secret $s' \in S$ was reconstructed, the node successfully terminates. If all $n - 1$ shares were received and an invalid secret $s' \in \mathbb{F} \setminus S$ is reconstructed it proceeds to the next iteration. In any other cases set all_honest := false and proceed.

In [77] the authors show that the protocol constitutes a Nash equilibrium which survives iterated deletion of weakly dominated strategies, if β is set accordingly. Note that the protocol does not explicitly terminate, but as soon as one party fails to broadcast her share, all other party also stop broadcasting and the protocol stalls. Similar protocols and results were concurrently presented by [1] and [101].

In summary, the game theoretic view of rational secret sharing can give interesting insights in situations where share holders have to be incentivized to participate in secret reconstruction or to provide true input for multiparty computation. However, the modelling of the parties' utility has a substantial influence on the result and cannot be done generically, but has to match the use case, e.g., as can be also seen from Desmedt and Slinko [55]. There are also not many use cases in the area of distributed storage where the model could be applied.

Social secret sharing as introduced by Nojoumian et al. [106] is a related concept which aims at managing trust levels of parties to quantify their expected behavior in a distributed fashion. The reputation for a node is derived by a trust function which combines the individual views about a party and ultimately assigns a weight to each party which is then subsequently used to distribute shares with a weighted secret sharing scheme [10]. The weights represent a party's reputation and are adjusted over time such that cooperative parties receive more shares compared to non-cooperative ones.

From a definitional point of view, social secret sharing extends threshold secret sharing by a social tuning function Tun which provides two main functionalities. Firstly, it updates the trust levels and subsequently computes new weights for share distribution. Secondly, it runs a form of proactive secret sharing to renew shares according to the updated weight distribution.

Although, the approach is interesting from a technical point of view its application is hard, due to the freedom in the design of appropriate trust function [86, 104]. Furthermore, the privacy aspect of secret sharing – which relies on the non-collusion assumption – is hard to capture in trust management, because colluding nodes cannot be identified by monitoring protocol behavior. In essence, for secure distributed cloud storage it seems a valid approach to optimize availability but not privacy.

Interestingly, although the two stands of social and rational secret sharing were developed independently, they have been also combined in [105] as socio-rational secret sharing.

Chapter 10
Conclusions

This work aims to provide an introduction to and overview of the different types of secret sharing schemes. To this end, we have presented a number of different techniques that have been shown to be secure in different models with limited and unlimited computational capabilities of the attacker. In particular, the information-theoretically secure solutions provide the highest levels of security with long-term security guarantees even against potential quantum attackers.

To maximize the information rate and to minimize the storage overhead, we have also analyzed computationally secure schemes, which, however, provide confidentiality guarantees only against limited attackers, but incur much lower memory overhead than their unconditionally secure counterparts. As a trade-off, also the notion of ramp secret sharing was reviewed. In practical applications, the specific choice will depend on the exact security requirements and classification level of the data to be used.

In addition to the power of the attackers, we also categorize the characteristics of the presented scheme for the network model used and the capabilities of the attackers at the protocol level. In particular, to cope with active attackers, we studied robust secret sharing schemes that provide integrity guarantees even when a limited number of nodes maliciously modify their shares. For storage solutions, as well as other higher-level cryptographic protocols, security against malicious dealers that may distribute inconsistent shares must also be considered, leading to the notion of verifiable secret sharing. Moreover, the notion of proactive secret sharing, where shares are renewed from time to time, also provides guarantees against mobile attackers who may corrupt various storage solutions over time, increasing the trust in long-term storage solutions.

Finally, we have presented advanced concepts for secret sharing, such as functional or social secret sharing, to give the reader a concise introduction and overview of the current state of the art.

We believe that this book can serve as an introduction to secret sharing without requiring strong prior mathematical or cryptographic knowledge. In addition, we hope that the overview will provide valuable guidance in choosing the right approach to secret sharing for a particular application scenario.

© The Author(s), under exclusive license to Springer Nature Switzerland AG 2023
S. Krenn and T. Lorünser, *An Introduction to Secret Sharing*,
SpringerBriefs in Information Security and Cryptography,
https://doi.org/10.1007/978-3-031-28161-7_10

References

1. Abraham, I., Dolev, D., Gonen, R., Halpern, J.Y.: Distributed computing meets game theory: robust mechanisms for rational secret sharing and multiparty computation. In: E. Ruppert, D. Malkhi (eds.) Proceedings of the Twenty-Fifth Annual ACM Symposium on Principles of Distributed Computing, PODC 2006, Denver, CO, USA, July 23-26, 2006, pp. 53–62. ACM (2006)
2. Backes, M., Kate, A., Patra, A.: Computational verifiable secret sharing revisited. In: D.H. Lee, X. Wang (eds.) Advances in Cryptology - ASIACRYPT 2011 - 17th International Conference on the Theory and Application of Cryptology and Information Security, Seoul, South Korea, December 4-8, 2011. Proceedings, *Lecture Notes in Computer Science*, vol. 7073, pp. 590–609. Springer (2011)
3. Ballico, E., Boato, G., Fontanari, C., Granelli, F.: Hierarchical Secret Sharing in Ad Hoc Networks Through Birkhoff Interpolation. In: Advances in Computer, Information, and Systems Sciences, and Engineering, pp. 157–164. Springer (2006)
4. Bangerter, E., Ghadafi, E., Krenn, S., Ahmad-Reza, S., Schneider, T., Smart, N., Warinschi, B.: Final Report on Unified Theoretical Framework of Efficient Zero-Knowledge Proofs of Knowledge. Project deliverable (2009). EU FP7 Project *CACE - Computer Aided Cryptography Engineering – D3.5*
5. Beaver, D.: Efficient multiparty protocols using circuit randomization. In: J. Feigenbaum (ed.) Advances in Cryptology - CRYPTO '91, 11th Annual International Cryptology Conference, Santa Barbara, California, USA, August 11-15, 1991, Proceedings, *Lecture Notes in Computer Science*, vol. 576, pp. 420–432. Springer (1991)
6. Bellare, M., Garay, J.A., Rabin, T.: Distributed pseudo-random bit generators - A new way to speed-up shared coin tossing. In: J.E. Burns, Y. Moses (eds.) Proceedings of the Fifteenth Annual ACM Symposium on Principles of Distributed Computing, Philadelphia, Pennsylvania, USA, May 23-26, 1996, pp. 191–200. ACM (1996)
7. Bellare, M., Goldreich, O.: On defining proofs of knowledge. In: E.F. Brickell (ed.) Advances in Cryptology - CRYPTO '92, 12th Annual International Cryptology Conference, Santa Barbara, California, USA, August 16-20, 1992, Proceedings, *Lecture Notes in Computer Science*, vol. 740, pp. 390–420. Springer (1992)
8. Ben-Or, M., Canetti, R., Goldreich, O.: Asynchronous secure computation. In: S.R. Kosaraju, D.S. Johnson, A. Aggarwal (eds.) Proceedings of the Twenty-Fifth Annual ACM Symposium on Theory of Computing, May 16-18, 1993, San Diego, CA, USA, pp. 52–61. ACM (1993)
9. Ben-Or, M., Goldwasser, S., Wigderson, A.: Completeness theorems for non-cryptographic fault-tolerant distributed computation (extended abstract). In: J. Simon (ed.) Proceedings of the 20th Annual ACM Symposium on Theory of Computing, May 2-4, 1988, Chicago, Illinois, USA, pp. 1–10. ACM (1988)
10. Benaloh, J.C., Leichter, J.: Generalized secret sharing and monotone functions. In: S. Goldwasser (ed.) Advances in Cryptology - CRYPTO '88, 8th Annual International Cryptology

© The Author(s), under exclusive license to Springer Nature Switzerland AG 2023
S. Krenn and T. Lorünser, *An Introduction to Secret Sharing*,
SpringerBriefs in Information Security and Cryptography,
https://doi.org/10.1007/978-3-031-28161-7

Conference, Santa Barbara, California, USA, August 21-25, 1988, Proceedings, *Lecture Notes in Computer Science*, vol. 403, pp. 27–35. Springer (1988)

11. Bessani, A.N., Correia, M.P., Quaresma, B., André, F., Sousa, P.: Depsky: dependable and secure storage in a cloud-of-clouds. In: C.M. Kirsch, G. Heiser (eds.) European Conference on Computer Systems, Proceedings of the Sixth European conference on Computer systems, EuroSys 2011, Salzburg, Austria, April 10-13, 2011, pp. 31–46. ACM (2011)

12. Bichsel, P., Camenisch, J., Dubovitskaya, M., Enderlein, R.E., Krenn, S., Lehmann, A., Neven, G., Preiss, F.S.: Cryptographic Protocols Underlying Privacy-ABCs. In: K. Rannenberg, J. Camenisch, A. Sabouri (eds.) Attribute-based Credentials for Trust. Springer (2015). EU FP7 Project *ABC4Trust - Attribute-based Credentials for Trust* – D8.15

13. Birkhoff, G.D.: General Mean Value and Remainder Theorems with Applications to Mechanical Differentiation and Quadrature. Transactions of the American Mathematical Society **7**(1) (1906)

14. Bishop, A., Pastro, V.: Robust secret sharing schemes against local adversaries. In: C. Cheng, K. Chung, G. Persiano, B. Yang (eds.) Public-Key Cryptography - PKC 2016 - 19th IACR International Conference on Practice and Theory in Public-Key Cryptography, Taipei, Taiwan, March 6-9, 2016, Proceedings, Part II, *Lecture Notes in Computer Science*, vol. 9615, pp. 327–356. Springer (2016)

15. Bishop, A., Pastro, V., Rajaraman, R., Wichs, D.: Essentially optimal robust secret sharing with maximal corruptions. In: M. Fischlin, J. Coron (eds.) Advances in Cryptology - EUROCRYPT 2016 - 35th Annual International Conference on the Theory and Applications of Cryptographic Techniques, Vienna, Austria, May 8-12, 2016, Proceedings, Part I, *Lecture Notes in Computer Science*, vol. 9665, pp. 58–86. Springer (2016)

16. Blakley, G.R.: Safeguarding cryptographic keys. In: 1979 International Workshop on Managing Requirements Knowledge, MARK 1979, New York, NY, USA, June 4-7, 1979, pp. 313–318. IEEE (1979)

17. Blakley, G.R., Meadows, C.A.: Security of ramp schemes. In: G.R. Blakley, D. Chaum (eds.) Advances in Cryptology, Proceedings of CRYPTO '84, Santa Barbara, California, USA, August 19-22, 1984, Proceedings, *Lecture Notes in Computer Science*, vol. 196, pp. 242–268. Springer (1984)

18. Blaze, M., Bleumer, G., Strauss, M.: Divertible protocols and atomic proxy cryptography. In: K. Nyberg (ed.) Advances in Cryptology - EUROCRYPT '98, International Conference on the Theory and Application of Cryptographic Techniques, Espoo, Finland, May 31 - June 4, 1998, Proceeding, *Lecture Notes in Computer Science*, vol. 1403, pp. 127–144. Springer (1998)

19. den Boer, B.: A simple and key-economical unconditional authentication scheme. J. Comput. Secur. **2**, 65–72 (1993)

20. Bogdanov, D., Laur, S., Willemson, J.: Sharemind: A framework for fast privacy-preserving computations. In: S. Jajodia, J. López (eds.) Computer Security - ESORICS 2008, 13th European Symposium on Research in Computer Security, Málaga, Spain, October 6-8, 2008. Proceedings, *Lecture Notes in Computer Science*, vol. 5283, pp. 192–206. Springer (2008)

21. Boyle, E.: Recent advances in function and homomorphic secret sharing - (invited talk). In: A. Patra, N.P. Smart (eds.) Progress in Cryptology - INDOCRYPT 2017 - 18th International Conference on Cryptology in India, Chennai, India, December 10-13, 2017, Proceedings, *Lecture Notes in Computer Science*, vol. 10698, pp. 1–26. Springer (2017)

22. Boyle, E., Chandran, N., Gilboa, N., Gupta, D., Ishai, Y., Kumar, N., Rathee, M.: Function secret sharing for mixed-mode and fixed-point secure computation. In: A. Canteaut, F. Standaert (eds.) Advances in Cryptology - EUROCRYPT 2021 - 40th Annual International Conference on the Theory and Applications of Cryptographic Techniques, Zagreb, Croatia, October 17-21, 2021, Proceedings, Part II, *Lecture Notes in Computer Science*, vol. 12697, pp. 871–900. Springer (2021)

23. Boyle, E., Couteau, G., Gilboa, N., Ishai, Y., Orrù, M.: Homomorphic secret sharing: Optimizations and applications. In: B. Thuraisingham, D. Evans, T. Malkin, D. Xu (eds.) Proceedings of the 2017 ACM SIGSAC Conference on Computer and Communications Se-

curity, CCS 2017, Dallas, TX, USA, October 30 - November 03, 2017, pp. 2105–2122. ACM (2017)

24. Boyle, E., Gilboa, N., Ishai, Y.: Function secret sharing. In: E. Oswald, M. Fischlin (eds.) Advances in Cryptology - EUROCRYPT 2015 - 34th Annual International Conference on the Theory and Applications of Cryptographic Techniques, Sofia, Bulgaria, April 26-30, 2015, Proceedings, Part II, *Lecture Notes in Computer Science*, vol. 9057, pp. 337–367. Springer (2015)

25. Boyle, E., Gilboa, N., Ishai, Y.: Breaking the circuit size barrier for secure computation under DDH. In: M. Robshaw, J. Katz (eds.) Advances in Cryptology - CRYPTO 2016 - 36th Annual International Cryptology Conference, Santa Barbara, CA, USA, August 14-18, 2016, Proceedings, Part I, *Lecture Notes in Computer Science*, vol. 9814, pp. 509–539. Springer (2016)

26. Boyle, E., Gilboa, N., Ishai, Y.: Function secret sharing: Improvements and extensions. In: E.R. Weippl, S. Katzenbeisser, C. Kruegel, A.C. Myers, S. Halevi (eds.) Proceedings of the 2016 ACM SIGSAC Conference on Computer and Communications Security, Vienna, Austria, October 24-28, 2016, pp. 1292–1303. ACM (2016)

27. Boyle, E., Gilboa, N., Ishai, Y.: Secure computation with preprocessing via function secret sharing. In: D. Hofheinz, A. Rosen (eds.) Theory of Cryptography - 17th International Conference, TCC 2019, Nuremberg, Germany, December 1-5, 2019, Proceedings, Part I, *Lecture Notes in Computer Science*, vol. 11891, pp. 341–371. Springer (2019)

28. Boyle, E., Gilboa, N., Ishai, Y., Lin, H., Tessaro, S.: Foundations of homomorphic secret sharing. In: A.R. Karlin (ed.) 9th Innovations in Theoretical Computer Science Conference, ITCS 2018, January 11-14, 2018, Cambridge, MA, USA, *LIPIcs*, vol. 94, pp. 21:1–21:21. Schloss Dagstuhl - Leibniz-Zentrum für Informatik (2018)

29. Boyle, E., Kohl, L., Scholl, P.: Homomorphic secret sharing from lattices without FHE. In: Y. Ishai, V. Rijmen (eds.) Advances in Cryptology - EUROCRYPT 2019 - 38th Annual International Conference on the Theory and Applications of Cryptographic Techniques, Darmstadt, Germany, May 19-23, 2019, Proceedings, Part II, *Lecture Notes in Computer Science*, vol. 11477, pp. 3–33. Springer (2019)

30. Brickell, E.F.: Some ideal secret sharing schemes. In: J. Quisquater, J. Vandewalle (eds.) Advances in Cryptology - EUROCRYPT '89, Workshop on the Theory and Application of of Cryptographic Techniques, Houthalen, Belgium, April 10-13, 1989, Proceedings, *Lecture Notes in Computer Science*, vol. 434, pp. 468–475. Springer (1989)

31. Cachin, C., Kursawe, K., Lysyanskaya, A., Strobl, R.: Asynchronous verifiable secret sharing and proactive cryptosystems. In: V. Atluri (ed.) Proceedings of the 9th ACM Conference on Computer and Communications Security, CCS 2002, Washington, DC, USA, November 18-22, 2002, pp. 88–97. ACM (2002)

32. Camenisch, J., Kiayias, A., Yung, M.: On the portability of generalized schnorr proofs. In: A. Joux (ed.) Advances in Cryptology - EUROCRYPT 2009, 28th Annual International Conference on the Theory and Applications of Cryptographic Techniques, Cologne, Germany, April 26-30, 2009. Proceedings, *Lecture Notes in Computer Science*, vol. 5479, pp. 425–442. Springer (2009)

33. Camenisch, J., Stadler, M.: Efficient group signature schemes for large groups (extended abstract). In: B.S.K. Jr. (ed.) Advances in Cryptology - CRYPTO '97, 17th Annual International Cryptology Conference, Santa Barbara, California, USA, August 17-21, 1997, Proceedings, *Lecture Notes in Computer Science*, vol. 1294, pp. 410–424. Springer (1997)

34. Canetti, R.: Studies in Secure Multiparty Computation and Applications. Ph.D. thesis, The Weizmann Institute of Science, Israel (1996)

35. Canetti, R., Rabin, T.: Fast asynchronous byzantine agreement with optimal resilience. In: S.R. Kosaraju, D.S. Johnson, A. Aggarwal (eds.) Proceedings of the Twenty-Fifth Annual ACM Symposium on Theory of Computing, May 16-18, 1993, San Diego, CA, USA, pp. 42–51. ACM (1993)

36. Carpentieri, M., Santis, A.D., Vaccaro, U.: Size of shares and probability of cheating in threshold schemes. In: T. Helleseth (ed.) Advances in Cryptology - EUROCRYPT '93,

Workshop on the Theory and Application of of Cryptographic Techniques, Lofthus, Norway, May 23-27, 1993, Proceedings, *Lecture Notes in Computer Science*, vol. 765, pp. 118–125. Springer (1993)

37. de Castro, L., Polychroniadou, A.: Lightweight, maliciously secure verifiable function secret sharing. In: O. Dunkelman, S. Dziembowski (eds.) Advances in Cryptology - EUROCRYPT 2022 - 41st Annual International Conference on the Theory and Applications of Cryptographic Techniques, Trondheim, Norway, May 30 - June 3, 2022, Proceedings, Part I, *Lecture Notes in Computer Science*, vol. 13275, pp. 150–179. Springer (2022)

38. Cevallos, A., Fehr, S., Ostrovsky, R., Rabani, Y.: Unconditionally-secure robust secret sharing with compact shares. In: D. Pointcheval, T. Johansson (eds.) Advances in Cryptology - EUROCRYPT 2012 - 31st Annual International Conference on the Theory and Applications of Cryptographic Techniques, Cambridge, UK, April 15-19, 2012. Proceedings, *Lecture Notes in Computer Science*, vol. 7237, pp. 195–208. Springer (2012)

39. Chandramouli, A., Choudhury, A., Patra, A.: A survey on perfectly-secure verifiable secret-sharing. IACR Cryptol. ePrint Arch. p. 445 (2021). URL https://eprint.iacr.org/2021/445

40. Chang, C., Lin, C., Lee, W., Hwang, P.: Secret sharing with access structures in a hierarchy. In: 18th International Conference on Advanced Information Networking and Applications (AINA 2004), 29-31 March 2004, Fukuoka, Japan, pp. 31–34. IEEE Computer Society (2004)

41. Charnes, C., Martin, K.M., Pieprzyk, J., Safavi-Naini, R.: Secret sharing in hierarchical groups. In: Y. Han, T. Okamoto, S. Qing (eds.) Information and Communication Security, First International Conference, ICICS'97, Beijing, China, November 11-14, 1997, Proceedings, *Lecture Notes in Computer Science*, vol. 1334, pp. 81–86. Springer (1997)

42. Chaum, D., Crépeau, C., Damgård, I.: Multiparty unconditionally secure protocols (extended abstract). In: J. Simon (ed.) Proceedings of the 20th Annual ACM Symposium on Theory of Computing, May 2-4, 1988, Chicago, Illinois, USA, pp. 11–19. ACM (1988)

43. Chen, K.: Authentication in a reconfigurable byzantine fault tolerant system. Master's thesis, Massachusetts Institute of Technology (2004)

44. Cheraghchi, M.: Nearly optimal robust secret sharing. In: IEEE International Symposium on Information Theory, ISIT 2016, Barcelona, Spain, July 10-15, 2016, pp. 2509–2513. IEEE (2016)

45. Chor, B., Goldwasser, S., Micali, S., Awerbuch, B.: Verifiable secret sharing and achieving simultaneity in the presence of faults (extended abstract). In: 26th Annual Symposium on Foundations of Computer Science, Portland, Oregon, USA, 21-23 October 1985, pp. 383–395. IEEE Computer Society (1985)

46. Choudhury, A., Hirt, M., Patra, A.: Asynchronous multiparty computation with linear communication complexity. In: Y. Afek (ed.) Distributed Computing - 27th International Symposium, DISC 2013, Jerusalem, Israel, October 14-18, 2013. Proceedings, *Lecture Notes in Computer Science*, vol. 8205, pp. 388–402. Springer (2013)

47. Cloud-of-clouds: DepSky by cloud-of-clouds. http://cloud-of-clouds.github.io/depsky/ (2015). Accessed: 2023-01-11

48. Cramer, R., Damgård, I., Fehr, S.: On the cost of reconstructing a secret, or VSS with optimal reconstruction phase. In: J. Kilian (ed.) Advances in Cryptology - CRYPTO 2001, 21st Annual International Cryptology Conference, Santa Barbara, California, USA, August 19-23, 2001, Proceedings, *Lecture Notes in Computer Science*, vol. 2139, pp. 503–523. Springer (2001)

49. Cramer, R., Damgård, I.B., Döttling, N., Fehr, S., Spini, G.: Linear secret sharing schemes from error correcting codes and universal hash functions. In: E. Oswald, M. Fischlin (eds.) Advances in Cryptology - EUROCRYPT 2015 - 34th Annual International Conference on the Theory and Applications of Cryptographic Techniques, Sofia, Bulgaria, April 26-30, 2015, Proceedings, Part II, *Lecture Notes in Computer Science*, vol. 9057, pp. 313–336. Springer (2015)

50. Damgård, I., Fujisaki, E.: A statistically-hiding integer commitment scheme based on groups with hidden order. In: Y. Zheng (ed.) Advances in Cryptology - ASIACRYPT 2002, 8th

International Conference on the Theory and Application of Cryptology and Information Security, Queenstown, New Zealand, December 1-5, 2002, Proceedings, *Lecture Notes in Computer Science*, vol. 2501, pp. 125–142. Springer (2002)

51. Damgård, I., Keller, M., Larraia, E., Pastro, V., Scholl, P., Smart, N.P.: Practical covertly secure MPC for dishonest majority - or: Breaking the SPDZ limits. In: J. Crampton, S. Jajodia, K. Mayes (eds.) Computer Security - ESORICS 2013 - 18th European Symposium on Research in Computer Security, Egham, UK, September 9-13, 2013. Proceedings, *Lecture Notes in Computer Science*, vol. 8134, pp. 1–18. Springer (2013)

52. Damgård, I., Pastro, V., Smart, N.P., Zakarias, S.: Multiparty computation from somewhat homomorphic encryption. In: R. Safavi-Naini, R. Canetti (eds.) Advances in Cryptology - CRYPTO 2012 - 32nd Annual Cryptology Conference, Santa Barbara, CA, USA, August 19-23, 2012. Proceedings, *Lecture Notes in Computer Science*, vol. 7417, pp. 643–662. Springer (2012)

53. Demirel, D., Krenn, S., Lorünser, T., Traverso, G.: Efficient and privacy preserving third party auditing for a distributed storage system. In: 11th International Conference on Availability, Reliability and Security, ARES 2016, Salzburg, Austria, August 31 - September 2, 2016, pp. 88–97. IEEE Computer Society (2016)

54. Desmedt, Y., Jajodia, S.: Redistributing secret shares to new access structures and its applications (1997)

55. Desmedt, Y., Slinko, A.: Realistic versus rational secret sharing. In: T. Alpcan, Y. Vorobeychik, J.S. Baras, G. Dán (eds.) Decision and Game Theory for Security - 10th International Conference, GameSec 2019, Stockholm, Sweden, October 30 - November 1, 2019, Proceedings, *Lecture Notes in Computer Science*, vol. 11836, pp. 152–163. Springer (2019)

56. Dinur, I., Keller, N., Klein, O.: An optimal distributed discrete log protocol with applications to homomorphic secret sharing. In: H. Shacham, A. Boldyreva (eds.) Advances in Cryptology - CRYPTO 2018 - 38th Annual International Cryptology Conference, Santa Barbara, CA, USA, August 19-23, 2018, Proceedings, Part III, *Lecture Notes in Computer Science*, vol. 10993, pp. 213–242. Springer (2018)

57. Dodis, Y., Halevi, S., Rothblum, R.D., Wichs, D.: Spooky encryption and its applications. In: M. Robshaw, J. Katz (eds.) Advances in Cryptology - CRYPTO 2016 - 36th Annual International Cryptology Conference, Santa Barbara, CA, USA, August 14-18, 2016, Proceedings, Part III, *Lecture Notes in Computer Science*, vol. 9816, pp. 93–122. Springer (2016)

58. Dolev, D., Dwork, C., Waarts, O., Yung, M.: Perfectly Secure Message Transmission. Journal of the ACM **40**(1), 17–47 (1993)

59. Eriguchi, R., Kunihiro, N.: Strongly secure ramp secret sharing schemes from any linear secret sharing schemes. In: 2019 IEEE Information Theory Workshop, ITW 2019, Visby, Sweden, August 25-28, 2019, pp. 1–5. IEEE (2019)

60. Eriguchi, R., Kunihiro, N.: Strong security of linear ramp secret sharing schemes with general access structures. Inf. Process. Lett. **164**, 106018 (2020)

61. Farràs, O., Padró, C.: Ideal hierarchical secret sharing schemes. In: D. Micciancio (ed.) Theory of Cryptography, 7th Theory of Cryptography Conference, TCC 2010, Zurich, Switzerland, February 9-11, 2010. Proceedings, *Lecture Notes in Computer Science*, vol. 5978, pp. 219–236. Springer (2010)

62. Fazio, N., Gennaro, R., Jafarikhah, T., III, W.E.S.: Homomorphic secret sharing from paillier encryption. In: T. Okamoto, Y. Yu, M.H. Au, Y. Li (eds.) Provable Security - 11th International Conference, ProvSec 2017, Xi'an, China, October 23-25, 2017, Proceedings, *Lecture Notes in Computer Science*, vol. 10592, pp. 381–399. Springer (2017)

63. Fehr, S., Yuan, C.: Towards optimal robust secret sharing with security against a rushing adversary. In: Y. Ishai, V. Rijmen (eds.) Advances in Cryptology - EUROCRYPT 2019 - 38th Annual International Conference on the Theory and Applications of Cryptographic Techniques, Darmstadt, Germany, May 19-23, 2019, Proceedings, Part III, *Lecture Notes in Computer Science*, vol. 11478, pp. 472–499. Springer (2019)

64. Feldman, P.: A practical scheme for non-interactive verifiable secret sharing. In: 28th Annual Symposium on Foundations of Computer Science, Los Angeles, California, USA, 27-29 October 1987, pp. 427–437. IEEE Computer Society (1987)

65. Fiat, A., Shamir, A.: How to prove yourself: Practical solutions to identification and signature problems. In: A.M. Odlyzko (ed.) Advances in Cryptology - CRYPTO '86, Santa Barbara, California, USA, 1986, Proceedings, *Lecture Notes in Computer Science*, vol. 263, pp. 186–194. Springer (1986)

66. Fitzi, M., Garay, J.A., Gollakota, S., Rangan, C.P., Srinathan, K.: Round-optimal and efficient verifiable secret sharing. In: S. Halevi, T. Rabin (eds.) Theory of Cryptography, Third Theory of Cryptography Conference, TCC 2006, New York, NY, USA, March 4-7, 2006, Proceedings, *Lecture Notes in Computer Science*, vol. 3876, pp. 329–342. Springer (2006)

67. Framner, E., Fischer-Hübner, S., Lorünser, T., Alaqra, A.S., Pettersson, J.S.: Making secret sharing based cloud storage usable. Inf. Comput. Secur. **27**(5) (2019)

68. Fujisaki, E., Okamoto, T.: Statistical zero knowledge protocols to prove modular polynomial relations. In: B.S.K. Jr. (ed.) Advances in Cryptology - CRYPTO '97, 17th Annual International Cryptology Conference, Santa Barbara, California, USA, August 17-21, 1997, Proceedings, *Lecture Notes in Computer Science*, vol. 1294, pp. 16–30. Springer (1997)

69. Fujisaki, E., Okamoto, T.: A practical and provably secure scheme for publicly verifiable secret sharing and its applications. In: K. Nyberg (ed.) Advances in Cryptology - EUROCRYPT '98, International Conference on the Theory and Application of Cryptographic Techniques, Espoo, Finland, May 31 - June 4, 1998, Proceeding, *Lecture Notes in Computer Science*, vol. 1403, pp. 32–46. Springer (1998)

70. Gamal, T.E.: A public key cryptosystem and a signature scheme based on discrete logarithms. In: G.R. Blakley, D. Chaum (eds.) Advances in Cryptology, Proceedings of CRYPTO '84, Santa Barbara, California, USA, August 19-22, 1984, Proceedings, *Lecture Notes in Computer Science*, vol. 196, pp. 10–18. Springer (1984)

71. Gennaro, R., Ishai, Y., Kushilevitz, E., Rabin, T.: The round complexity of verifiable secret sharing and secure multicast. In: J.S. Vitter, P.G. Spirakis, M. Yannakakis (eds.) Proceedings on 33rd Annual ACM Symposium on Theory of Computing, July 6-8, 2001, Heraklion, Crete, Greece, pp. 580–589. ACM (2001)

72. Gentry, C.: A fully homomorphic encryption scheme. Ph.D. thesis, Stanford University, USA (2009)

73. Ghodosi, H., Pieprzyk, J., Safavi-Naini, R.: Secret sharing in multilevel and compartmented groups. In: C. Boyd, E. Dawson (eds.) Information Security and Privacy, Third Australasian Conference, ACISP'98, Brisbane, Queensland, Australia, July 1998, Proceedings, *Lecture Notes in Computer Science*, vol. 1438, pp. 367–378. Springer (1998)

74. Gilboa, N., Ishai, Y.: Distributed point functions and their applications. In: P.Q. Nguyen, E. Oswald (eds.) Advances in Cryptology - EUROCRYPT 2014 - 33rd Annual International Conference on the Theory and Applications of Cryptographic Techniques, Copenhagen, Denmark, May 11-15, 2014. Proceedings, *Lecture Notes in Computer Science*, vol. 8441, pp. 640–658. Springer (2014)

75. Giry, D.: Keylength - Cryptographic Key Length Recommendation. `http://www.keylength.com/` (2015). Accessed: 2023-01-11

76. Goldwasser, S., Micali, S., Rackoff, C.: The knowledge complexity of interactive proof-systems (extended abstract). In: R. Sedgewick (ed.) Proceedings of the 17th Annual ACM Symposium on Theory of Computing, May 6-8, 1985, Providence, Rhode Island, USA, pp. 291–304. ACM (1985)

77. Gordon, S.D., Katz, J.: Rational secret sharing, revisited. In: R.D. Prisco, M. Yung (eds.) Security and Cryptography for Networks, 5th International Conference, SCN 2006, Maiori, Italy, September 6-8, 2006, Proceedings, *Lecture Notes in Computer Science*, vol. 4116, pp. 229–241. Springer (2006)

78. Gupta, V.H., Gopinath, K.: An extended verifiable secret redistribution protocol for archival systems. In: Proceedings of the The First International Conference on Availability, Reliability and Security, ARES 2006, The International Dependability Conference - Bridging Theory and Practice, April 20-22 2006, Vienna University of Technology, Austria, pp. 100–107. IEEE Computer Society (2006)

79. Gupta, V.H., Gopinath, K.: $G_{its}{}^2$ VSR: an information theoretical secure verifiable secret redistribution protocol for long-term archival storage. In: Fourth International IEEE Security

in Storage Workshop, SISW 2007, San Diego, California, USA, September 27, 2007, pp. 22–33. IEEE Computer Society (2007)

80. Halpern, J.Y., Teague, V.: Rational secret sharing and multiparty computation: extended abstract. In: L. Babai (ed.) Proceedings of the 36th Annual ACM Symposium on Theory of Computing, Chicago, IL, USA, June 13-16, 2004, pp. 623–632. ACM (2004)

81. Happe, A., Wohner, F., Lorünser, T.: The Archistar secret-sharing backup proxy. In: Proceedings of the 12th International Conference on Availability, Reliability and Security, Reggio Calabria, Italy, August 29 - September 01, 2017, pp. 88:1–88:8. ACM (2017)

82. Herzberg, A., Jarecki, S., Krawczyk, H., Yung, M.: Proactive secret sharing or: How to cope with perpetual leakage. In: D. Coppersmith (ed.) Advances in Cryptology - CRYPTO '95, 15th Annual International Cryptology Conference, Santa Barbara, California, USA, August 27-31, 1995, Proceedings, *Lecture Notes in Computer Science*, vol. 963, pp. 339–352. Springer (1995)

83. Ito, M., Saito, A., Nishizeki, T.: Secret Sharing Scheme Realizing General Access Structure. Electronics and Communications in Japan (Part III: Fundamental Electronic Science) **72**(9), 56–64 (1989)

84. Iwamoto, M., Yamamoto, H.: Strongly secure ramp secret sharing schemes for general access structures. Inf. Process. Lett. **97**(2), 52–57 (2006)

85. Jhanwar, M.P., Venkateswarlu, A., Safavi-Naini, R.: Paillier-Based Publicly Verifiable (Non-Interactive) Secret Sharing. Designs, Codes and Cryptography **73**(2), 529–546 (2014)

86. Jøsang, A., Ismail, R., Boyd, C.: A survey of trust and reputation systems for online service provision. Decis. Support Syst. **43**(2), 618–644 (2007)

87. Käsper, E., Nikov, V., Nikova, S.: Strongly Multiplicative Hierarchical Threshold Secret Sharing. In: Information Theoretic Security, pp. 148–168. Springer (2009)

88. Katz, J., Koo, C., Kumaresan, R.: Improving the round complexity of VSS in point-to-point networks. In: L. Aceto, I. Damgård, L.A. Goldberg, M.M. Halldórsson, A. Ingólfsdóttir, I. Walukiewicz (eds.) Automata, Languages and Programming, 35th International Colloquium, ICALP 2008, Reykjavik, Iceland, July 7-11, 2008, Proceedings, Part II - Track B: Logic, Semantics, and Theory of Programming & Track C: Security and Cryptography Foundations, *Lecture Notes in Computer Science*, vol. 5126, pp. 499–510. Springer (2008)

89. Katz, J., Lindell, Y.: Introduction to Modern Cryptography, Third Edition. CRC Press (2020)

90. Koch, K., Krenn, S., Marc, T., More, S., Ramacher, S.: KRAKEN: a privacy-preserving data market for authentic data. In: N. Laoutaris, M. Mellia (eds.) Proceedings of the 1st International Workshop on Data Economy, DE 2022, Rome, Italy, 9 December 2022, pp. 15–20. ACM (2022)

91. Kothari, S.C.: Generalized linear threshold scheme. In: G.R. Blakley, D. Chaum (eds.) Advances in Cryptology, Proceedings of CRYPTO '84, Santa Barbara, California, USA, August 19-22, 1984, Proceedings, *Lecture Notes in Computer Science*, vol. 196, pp. 231–241. Springer (1984)

92. Krawczyk, H.: Distributed fingerprints and secure information dispersal. In: J. Anderson, S. Toueg (eds.) Proceedings of the Twelth Annual ACM Symposium on Principles of Distributed Computing, Ithaca, New York, USA, August 15-18, 1993, pp. 207–218. ACM (1993)

93. Krawczyk, H.: Secret sharing made short. In: D.R. Stinson (ed.) Advances in Cryptology - CRYPTO '93, 13th Annual International Cryptology Conference, Santa Barbara, California, USA, August 22-26, 1993, Proceedings, *Lecture Notes in Computer Science*, vol. 773, pp. 136–146. Springer (1993)

94. Krenn, S., Lorünser, T., Striecks, C.: Batch-verifiable secret sharing with unconditional privacy. In: P. Mori, S. Furnell, O. Camp (eds.) Proceedings of the 3rd International Conference on Information Systems Security and Privacy, ICISSP 2017, Porto, Portugal, February 19-21, 2017, pp. 303–311. SciTePress (2017)

95. Kurosawa, K., Suzuki, K.: Almost secure (1-round, *n*-channel) message transmission scheme. IEICE Trans. Fundam. Electron. Commun. Comput. Sci. **92-A**(1), 105–112 (2009)

96. Lamport, L., Shostak, R.E., Pease, M.C.: The byzantine generals problem. ACM Trans. Program. Lang. Syst. **4**(3), 382–401 (1982)

97. Lorünser, T., Happe, A., Rainer, B., Wohner, F., Striecks, C., Demirel, D., Traverso, G.: Advanced architecture for distributed storage in dynamic environments (SECOSTOR Tool). Project deliverable (2017). EU H2020 Project *PRISMACLOUD - PRIvacy & Security MAintaining Services in the CLOUD* – D5.1

98. Lorünser, T., Happe, A., Slamanig, D.: ARCHISTAR: towards secure and robust cloud based data sharing. In: 7th IEEE International Conference on Cloud Computing Technology and Science, CloudCom 2015, Vancouver, BC, Canada, November 30 - December 3, 2015, pp. 371–378. IEEE Computer Society (2015)

99. Lorünser, T., Wohner, F., Krenn, S.: A privacy-preserving auction platform with public verifiability for smart manufacturing. In: P. Mori, G. Lenzini, S. Furnell (eds.) Proceedings of the 8th International Conference on Information Systems Security and Privacy, ICISSP 2022, Online Streaming, February 9-11, 2022, pp. 637–647. SCITEPRESS (2022)

100. Lorünser, T., Wohner, F., Krenn, S.: A verifiable multiparty computation solver for the linear assignment problem: And applications to air traffic management. In: F. Regazzoni, M. van Dijk (eds.) Proceedings of the 2022 on Cloud Computing Security Workshop, CCSW 2022, Los Angeles, CA, USA, 7 November 2022, pp. 41–51. ACM (2022)

101. Lysyanskaya, A., Triandopoulos, N.: Rationality and adversarial behavior in multi-party computation. In: C. Dwork (ed.) Advances in Cryptology - CRYPTO 2006, 26th Annual International Cryptology Conference, Santa Barbara, California, USA, August 20-24, 2006, Proceedings, *Lecture Notes in Computer Science*, vol. 4117, pp. 180–197. Springer (2006)

102. Manurangsi, P., Srinivasan, A., Vasudevan, P.N.: Nearly optimal robust secret sharing against rushing adversaries. In: D. Micciancio, T. Ristenpart (eds.) Advances in Cryptology - CRYPTO 2020 - 40th Annual International Cryptology Conference, CRYPTO 2020, Santa Barbara, CA, USA, August 17-21, 2020, Proceedings, Part III, *Lecture Notes in Computer Science*, vol. 12172, pp. 156–185. Springer (2020)

103. Naskar, R., Sengupta, I.: Secret Sharing and Proactive Renewal of Shares in Hierarchical Groups. CoRR **abs/1006.1192** (2010). URL http://arxiv.org/abs/1006.1192

104. Nojoumian, M., Stinson, D.R.: Social secret sharing in cloud computing using a new trust function. In: N. Cuppens-Boulahia, P. Fong, J. García-Alfaro, S. Marsh, J. Steghöfer (eds.) Tenth Annual International Conference on Privacy, Security and Trust, PST 2012, Paris, France, July 16-18, 2012, pp. 161–167. IEEE Computer Society (2012)

105. Nojoumian, M., Stinson, D.R.: Socio-rational secret sharing as a new direction in rational cryptography. In: J. Grosssklags, J.C. Walrand (eds.) Decision and Game Theory for Security - Third International Conference, GameSec 2012, Budapest, Hungary, November 5-6, 2012. Proceedings, *Lecture Notes in Computer Science*, vol. 7638, pp. 18–37. Springer (2012)

106. Nojoumian, M., Stinson, D.R., Grainger, M.: Unconditionally secure social secret sharing scheme. IET Inf. Secur. **4**(4), 202–211 (2010)

107. Ostrovsky, R., Yung, M.: How to withstand mobile virus attacks (extended abstract). In: L. Logrippo (ed.) Proceedings of the Tenth Annual ACM Symposium on Principles of Distributed Computing, Montreal, Quebec, Canada, August 19-21, 1991, pp. 51–59. ACM (1991)

108. Patra, A., Choudhary, A., Rangan, C.P.: Efficient statistical asynchronous verifiable secret sharing with optimal resilience. In: K. Kurosawa (ed.) Information Theoretic Security, 4th International Conference, ICITS 2009, Shizuoka, Japan, December 3-6, 2009. Revised Selected Papers, *Lecture Notes in Computer Science*, vol. 5973, pp. 74–92. Springer (2009)

109. Patra, A., Choudhary, A., Rangan, C.P.: Simple and efficient asynchronous byzantine agreement with optimal resilience. In: S. Tirthapura, L. Alvisi (eds.) Proceedings of the 28th Annual ACM Symposium on Principles of Distributed Computing, PODC 2009, Calgary, Alberta, Canada, August 10-12, 2009, pp. 92–101. ACM (2009)

110. Patra, A., Choudhury, A., Rangan, C.P.: Efficient asynchronous verifiable secret sharing and multiparty computation. J. Cryptol. **28**(1), 49–109 (2015)

111. Pedersen, T.P.: Non-interactive and information-theoretic secure verifiable secret sharing. In: J. Feigenbaum (ed.) Advances in Cryptology - CRYPTO '91, 11th Annual International Cryptology Conference, Santa Barbara, California, USA, August 11-15, 1991, Proceedings, *Lecture Notes in Computer Science*, vol. 576, pp. 129–140. Springer (1991)

112. Rabin, M.O.: Efficient Dispersal of Information for Security, Load Balancing, and Fault Tolerance. Journal of the ACM **36**(2), 335–348 (1989)
113. Rabin, T., Ben-Or, M.: Verifiable secret sharing and multiparty protocols with honest majority (extended abstract). In: D.S. Johnson (ed.) Proceedings of the 21st Annual ACM Symposium on Theory of Computing, May 14-17, 1989, Seattle, Washington, USA, pp. 73–85. ACM (1989)
114. Rogaway, P., Bellare, M.: Robust computational secret sharing and a unified account of classical secret-sharing goals. In: P. Ning, S.D.C. di Vimercati, P.F. Syverson (eds.) Proceedings of the 2007 ACM Conference on Computer and Communications Security, CCS 2007, Alexandria, Virginia, USA, October 28-31, 2007, pp. 172–184. ACM (2007)
115. Rogaway, P., Shrimpton, T.: Cryptographic hash-function basics: Definitions, implications, and separations for preimage resistance, second-preimage resistance, and collision resistance. In: B.K. Roy, W. Meier (eds.) Fast Software Encryption, 11th International Workshop, FSE 2004, Delhi, India, February 5-7, 2004, Revised Papers, *Lecture Notes in Computer Science*, vol. 3017, pp. 371–388. Springer (2004)
116. Runhua, S., Hong, Z.: A Hierarchical Threshold Multi-Secret Sharing Scheme. In: Anti-Counterfeiting, Security and Identification - ASID 2008, pp. 231–234. IEEE (2008)
117. Sahai, A., Waters, B.: Fuzzy identity-based encryption. In: R. Cramer (ed.) Advances in Cryptology - EUROCRYPT 2005, 24th Annual International Conference on the Theory and Applications of Cryptographic Techniques, Aarhus, Denmark, May 22-26, 2005, Proceedings, *Lecture Notes in Computer Science*, vol. 3494, pp. 457–473. Springer (2005)
118. Schnorr, C.: Efficient Signature Generation by Smart Cards. J. Cryptol. **4**(3), 161–174 (1991)
119. Schoenmakers, B.: A simple publicly verifiable secret sharing scheme and its application to electronic. In: M.J. Wiener (ed.) Advances in Cryptology - CRYPTO '99, 19th Annual International Cryptology Conference, Santa Barbara, California, USA, August 15-19, 1999, Proceedings, *Lecture Notes in Computer Science*, vol. 1666, pp. 148–164. Springer (1999)
120. Schultz, D.A., Liskov, B., Liskov, M.: Mobile proactive secret sharing. In: Proceedings of the Twenty-Seventh Annual ACM Symposium on Principles of Distributed Computing, PODC 2008, Toronto, Canada, August 18-21, 2008, p. 458 (2008)
121. Schultz, D.A., Liskov, B., Liskov, M.: MPSS: mobile proactive secret sharing. ACM Trans. Inf. Syst. Secur. **13**(4), 34 (2010)
122. Selimi, M., Freitag, F.: Tahoe-lafs distributed storage service in community network clouds. In: 2014 IEEE Fourth International Conference on Big Data and Cloud Computing, BDCloud 2014, Sydney, Australia, December 3-5, 2014, pp. 17–24. IEEE Computer Society (2014)
123. Shamir, A.: How to Share a Secret. Commununications of the ACM **22**(11), 612–613 (1979)
124. Shor, P.W.: Polynomial-Time Algorithms for Prime Factorization and Discrete Logarithms on a Quantum Computer. SIAM Journal on Computing **26**(5), 1484–1509 (1997)
125. Simmons, G.J.: How to (really) share a secret. In: S. Goldwasser (ed.) Advances in Cryptology - CRYPTO '88, 8th Annual International Cryptology Conference, Santa Barbara, California, USA, August 21-25, 1988, Proceedings, *Lecture Notes in Computer Science*, vol. 403, pp. 390–448. Springer (1988)
126. Stangl, J., Lorünser, T., Dinakarrao, S.M.P.: A fast and resource efficient FPGA implementation of secret sharing for storage applications. In: J. Madsen, A.K. Coskun (eds.) 2018 Design, Automation & Test in Europe Conference & Exhibition, DATE 2018, Dresden, Germany, March 19-23, 2018, pp. 654–659. IEEE (2018)
127. Stinson, D.R., Wei, R.: Unconditionally secure proactive secret sharing scheme with combinatorial structures. In: H.M. Heys, C.M. Adams (eds.) Selected Areas in Cryptography, 6th Annual International Workshop, SAC'99, Kingston, Ontario, Canada, August 9-10, 1999, Proceedings, *Lecture Notes in Computer Science*, vol. 1758, pp. 200–214. Springer (1999)
128. Sun, H., Zheng, X., Yu, Y.: A Proactive Secret Sharing Scheme Based on Elliptic Curve Cryptography. In: Education Technology and Computer Science 2009, pp. 666–669 (2009)
129. Tassa, T.: Hierarchical Threshold Secret Sharing. J. Cryptol. **20**(2), 237–264 (2007)
130. Tassa, T., Dyn, N.: Multipartite Secret Sharing by Bivariate Interpolation. J. Cryptol. **22**(2), 227–258 (2009)

131. Tentu, A.N., Paul, P., Venkaiah, V.C.: Ideal and Perfect Hierarchical Secret Sharing Schemes based on MDS Codes. IACR Cryptology ePrint Archive **2013**, 189 (2013). URL http://eprint.iacr.org/2013/189

132. Tompa, M., Woll, H.: How to share a secret with cheaters. J. Cryptol. **1**(2), 133–138 (1988)

133. Traverso, G., Demirel, D., Buchmann, J.: Dynamic and verifiable hierarchical secret sharing. In: A.C.A. Nascimento, P.S.L.M. Barreto (eds.) Information Theoretic Security - 9th International Conference, ICITS 2016, Tacoma, WA, USA, August 9-12, 2016, Revised Selected Papers, *Lecture Notes in Computer Science*, vol. 10015, pp. 24–43 (2016)

134. Veldhorst, M., Yang, C.H., Hwang, J.C.C., Huang, W., Dehollain, J.P., Muhonen, J.T., Simmons, S., Laucht, A., Hudson, F.E., Itoh, K.M., Morello, A., Dzurak, A.S.: A two-qubit logic gate in silicon. Nature **526**, 410–414 (2015)

135. Welch, L., Berlekamp, E.: Error Correction of Algebraic Block Codes. US Patent #4,633,470 (1983)

136. Wong, T.M., Wang, C., Wing, J.M.: Verifiable secret redistribution for archive system. In: Proceedings of the First International IEEE Security in Storage Workshop, SISW 2002, Greenbelt, Maryland, USA, December 11, 2002, pp. 94–106. IEEE Computer Society (2002)

137. Yamamoto, H.: Secret sharing system using (k, l, n) threshold scheme. Electronics and Communications in Japan (Part I: Communications) **69**(9), 46–54 (1986)

138. Zhang, E., Li, M., Yiu, S., Du, J., Zhu, J., Jin, G.: Fair hierarchical secret sharing scheme based on smart contract. Inf. Sci. **546**, 166–176 (2021)

139. Zhao, C., Zhao, S., Zhao, M., Chen, Z., Gao, C., Li, H., Tan, Y.: Secure multi-party computation: Theory, practice and applications. Inf. Sci. **476**, 357–372 (2019)

140. Zhou, L., Schneider, F.B., van Renesse, R.: APSS: proactive secret sharing in asynchronous systems. ACM Trans. Inf. Syst. Secur. **8**(3), 259–286 (2005)

Printed in the United States
by Baker & Taylor Publisher Services